The
Southern Way

The regular volume for the Southern devotee

Kevin Robertson

Issue 46

© 2019 Crécy Publishing Ltd
and the various contributors

ISBN 9781909328877

First published in 2019 by Noodle Books
an imprint of Crécy Publishing Ltd

New contact details
All editorial submissions to:
The Southern Way (Kevin Robertson)
'Silmaril'
Upper Lambourn
Hungerford
Berkshire RG17 8QR
Tel: 01488 674143
editorial@thesouthernway.co.uk

A CIP record for this book is available from the British Library

Publisher's note: Every effort has been made to identify and correctly attribute photographic credits. Any error that may have occurred is entirely unintentional.

Printed in Malta by Gutenberg Press Limited

Noodle Books is an imprint of
Crécy Publishing Limited
1a Ringway Trading Estate
Shadowmoss Road
Manchester M22 5LH

www.crecy.co.uk

Issue No 47 of THE SOUTHERN WAY
ISBN 9781909328884
available in July 2019 at £14.95

To receive your copy the moment it is released, order in advance from your usual supplier, or it can be sent post-free (UK) direct from the publisher:

Crécy Publishing Ltd

1a Ringway Trading Estate, Shadowmoss Road, Manchester M22 5LH

Tel 0161 499 0024

www.crecy.co.uk

enquiries@crecy.co.uk

Front cover:
USA No 30070 out of use at Eastleigh alongside another member of the class. As No 30070, it was withdrawn from capital stock week-ending 6 October 1962 but was reinstated for departmental use in August 1963, being renumbered DS238. It survived, on paper at least, until September 1967 and as such was one of the final two steam engines on the books of the Southern Region (the other was sister engine DS237 formerly No 30065 of the same class). Both would end up in preservation, No 30070 finding a home on the Kent & East Sussex Railway.

Rear cover:
No 34006 *Bude* drifts into Dorchester South with a down Weymouth train on an unknown date. On the opposite side of the line the post carries the 'backing signal' for up trains, (by this time an elevated disc) which allowed Bournemouth bound trains to reverse into the dead-end up platform.

Title page:
Just to prove No 35028 'Clan line' was not always in the pristine condition in which she appears nowadays, she is seen here on a down Bournemouth line service at Worting Junction west of Basingstoke. (Ever wondered when a single distant signal such as shown here was used....well here is the example. On the right [as viewed] the stop and distant signals are 'on' and apply to the 'relief' line. The stop signal on the extreme left applies to both the 'fast' Salisbury line AND the Bournemouth line – the latter if the crossover is set. The fact the distant in the centre is 'off' confirms the train will take the crossover and of course the next stop signal is also 'off'.) *The late Tony Woodforth collection*

Contents

Introduction

As a student of railway history (I doubt any one of us ever 'graduates') it can be all too easy to concentrate on just the one, or a few aspects of railway history that have personal appeal.

Editing 'SW' over the years has been a real eye-opener in that respect, for far from thinking I was perhaps alone in having a specific interest in one or two aspects/areas, I quickly learned there were countless others with similar or diverse interests, either in the same or in the different geographical areas of the former SR.

Locomotives are (I suspect) right at the top of most peoples' lists, followed (it appears) by rolling stock (EMUs included) and then specific stations or routes; the latter were often born out of interest in a location that was familiar in childhood or a regular route/scene traversed.

We could of course sub-divide these and many other topics further, no doubt many times, but as Editor I do have to be a little bit careful not to venture too far into the really obscure. (So far no one has offered an article on 'SR Buffer Stops' or the like, but were it interesting, it could well be included!) As a brief aside, I might mention that I remember a few years ago, a time when I was regularly out selling books at shows most weekends, I put up a spoof 'Forthcoming Titles' list. This covered all regions but I took it down when someone tried ordering, 'LNER lavatory pans: Second-Class'. The message was clear: not everyone shares the same sense of humour.

What I know myself, and others have gleaned from 'SW' and other publications, is just how much there is to know that we were frankly not aware of. Hence you may have devoured all there is to know on say Mr Bulleid's steam creations but I can still promise there will be areas of railway history, operation that remain unknown.

One of these was pointed out to me recently by a very good friend who is currently researching, shall we say, 'another railway'. (He is a dear friend so I do not hold that against him.) What he told me though was fascinating and that was how much the railway companies charged to move coal and similarly how much was the demurrage charge to the consignee. (Demurrage is the 'standing/storage' charge applied to the recipient of a coal wagon if he does not unload it within 24hrs.) This cost in 1911 was ¼d (one-farthing) per ton / per mile. So a coal wagon carrying say 10 tons and travelling 150 miles from colliery to destination would cost the colliery/customer (dependent upon the arrangement for who paid) £1 11s 3d. A not inconsiderable sum, and perhaps explaining the obvious reason why coal was more expensive to buy, the further the distance it had to be transported from the pit head. Add to this a 6s demurrage charge per day and it can be seen why there was the incentive to unload the wagon as soon as possible. Before demurrage, merchants had been known to delay unloading; in effect using the railway coal wagon and the siding upon which it stood as a free storage facility to be drawn from only when required. (Contemporary reports record the pit-head price of 'first-class' coal was then 11s per ton, although as has been seen, carriage charges would triple this cost, using the example given, and that was just taking into account the time for it to reach the merchant, who in turn would need to add his own margin.)

This transport cost might seem excessive, indeed no doubt an argument could be made to prove the point, but it must be recalled that this was invariably one way traffic, coal wagons rarely used, or indeed suitable, for much in the way of a return load, and the railway had to factor this cost, that of running empty trains of wagons back to the colliery, into the equation. Whether the costs quoted referred to using 'private owner' or railway company vehicles is not explained.

We might also mention that to avoid this demurrage charge, a number of merchants established their own 'private sidings' where their own private owner wagons might sit peacefully and undisturbed to be unloaded at leisure. But then there was the cost of maintaining this facility! It was clearly not a 'get rich quick' scheme for most.

Concluding the above, if anyone would like to 'dig deep' (pun is deliberate), into the methods of, and movement of coal on the SR and its predecessors, I am sure it would be a most interesting read, especially as there were only a very few stations that did not have at least one coal merchant – a time when coal was the preferred method of heating and cooking for the majority of households in the land as well as being moved to local gasworks and supplied to business.

I will end this Editorial with a reminder to note that our postal address and telephone has changed. (Telephone calls are welcome, office hours only please, and on Editorial matters only, NOT sales or subscriptions. Please note the new area dialling code is also only one digit different to that previous but the geographical area is 50 miles from where we were before.) Email contact remains unaffected. The old 'PO Box' address is also now well and truly defunct.

Be assured we have not 'gone over to the dark side' as one commentator put it, more like 'come into the light' (literally) as we now have views over open countryside compared with the brick walls and back gardens as had been the case before.

Kevin Robertson

Opposite: **It could be in preservation days but rest assured it is not. Simply described as 'preparing for the road', a scene undertaken literally tens of thousands of times but how often recorded? (No details unfortunately of when, where, who, or what.)**

LSWR Locomotive Class Designations

George Hobbs

(Following much debate regarding 'Why' and 'What', we are delighted to include this short article which should explain all.)

At first sight the class designations assigned to LSWR locomotives may seem illogical. When William Adams joined the LSWR from the Great Eastern in 1878 he introduced a Works Order system, similar to that of his previous employer. Works Order numbers applied to jobs carried out in the railway's own works, including the construction of engines: starting at 'A1', the numbers progressed through 'B1', 'C1', etc., continuing the sequence through 'A2', 'B2', and so on. Letters 'I', 'J', 'Q', 'U', 'W', and 'Z' were not used. For a new locomotive design the Works Order also became the class name.

Not all Works Orders related to locomotive construction, for example tenders were constructed under separate orders, so there are considerable gaps in the sequence when only locomotive classes are considered. In general the class names indicate their chronology, if little else. For successful designs subsequent batches were allocated to the same class as the first batch, even though their Works Order numbers were different. This avoided the possibility of otherwise practically identical engines belonging to several different classes and the consequent confusion in the operating divisions.

The main drawback with the system was the lack of any apparent connection between locomotives that were similar but with relatively minor variations. An example of this would be the ten 4-4-0 engines of Drummond's class 'C8' (1898), whose design was modified by extending the coupled wheelbase and the boiler by a foot to produce the more well known and prolific, but apparently unrelated, 'T9' class. Various batches of the 'T9' also showed detailed differences, such as water tube fireboxes, cab and splasher widths, but which were not sufficient to lead to the introduction of a new class.

The final Urie classes were the Feltham 4-8-0T hump shunters of class 'G16' and the heavy freight 4-6-2T of class 'H16' of 1921. As the LSWR class naming system ceased for new classes with railway grouping in 1923, these were the final application of this system.

The familiar classes of 4-6-0 with different driving wheel diameters for mixed traffic ('H15', 6'-0" wheels, 1914), express

The USA class found their main employment at works/sheds shunting engines and of course also at Southampton Docks. Here No 30064 pushes a rake of wagons between the shops at the Eastleigh carriage works, a group of men seemingly waiting for the move to be completed before venturing across. Alongside is newly refurbished DEMU No 1109.

LSWR (Nine Elms) Order No 'F13' and consequently Class No 'F13' No 330 4-6-0, one of five machines of identical type to this order number. Some years later in 1924, order number 'A17' was allocated at Eastleigh to the same five engines as at the time of rebuilding into class 'H15' but retained the same engine numbers.

passenger ('N15', 6'-7" wheels, 1918) and freight ('S15', 5'-7" wheels, 1920) were among the later LSWR designs. The 'N15' and 'S15' classes were perpetuated by Maunsell post-grouping, although detail design changes were made. As a South Eastern man, Maunsell continued the existing SECR class system for his new designs for the Southern.

An anomaly was the Jubilee class of 0-4-2 which was assigned class 'A12' and appeared in batches between 1887 and 1894. This should probably have been 'A2' and this class contravenes the otherwise chronological sequence of identification.

To add to the confusion (?), some LSWR classes did not obey the above rules. The '700' class 0-6-0 goods engines (built by Dubs in 1897) and the '415'* class radial 4-4-2 tanks (initial batch by Beyer, Peacock in 1882, with subsequent batches from Neilson, Stephenson and Dubs) both fell outside the system. Although of LSWR design, they were not built in-house, so there was no Works Order number. Such engines were assigned a

* Why an '0' was added – by whom and when [?] – to make them '0415' is not reported.

class number instead of the alphanumeric code of their home grown brothers.

Subsequent batches of engines were assigned to the same class as the earlier examples, irrespective of their place of manufacture. Dubs built some of the 'T9's and the thirty "Scottish" King Arthurs supplied by the North British Locomotive Company to the Southern in 1925 were still 'N15's.

A final inconsistency arose after the Brighton line was electrified in 1933: the seven 4-6-4T locomotives of LBSCR class 'L' (*Remembrance* class), introduced in 1914, were rebuilt as 4-6-0 tender engines and reclassified as 'N15X'. The 'X' suffix having been a Brighton specialty to denote a rebuilt and, hopefully, improved variant. However these engines had never been 'N15's and apart from being 4-6-0s had little in common with either the LSWR or the Southern engines whose classification they had appropriated.

So there is some logic in the LSWR locomotive class names, even if it is not quite as transparent as that employed by most railways – except of course on the Great Eastern, whose system it was that had been copied.

Nine Elms order 'R9' was for a batch of five 'G6' 0-6-0T engines, Numbers 348/9/51/3/4; the first of the batch is seen here and was completed in May 1900.

Nine Elms Order Nos. 1887-1908

Order No	Loco Class	Loco type	Number in class	Original running numbers	Date of completion of first loco
E1	A12	0-4-2T	10	537-546	3/1888
T1	T1	0-4-4T	10	61-70	6/1888
D2	T1	0-4-4T	10	71-80	6/1889
M2	A12	0-4-2	10	547-556	6/1889
O2	O2	0-4-4T	10	177-186	12/1889
V2	X2	4-4-0	10	547-586	6/1890
B3	O2	0-4-4T	10	187-196	10/1890
F3	X2	4-4-0	10	587-596	10/1891
K3	O2	0-4-4T	10	197-206	6/1891
T3	T3	4-4-0	10	557-566	12/1892
B4	B4	0-4-0T	10	85-94	10/1891
D4	T1	0-4-4T	20	207-226	12/1891
O4	A12	0-4-2	10	597-606	12/1893
S5	T3	4-4-0	10	567-576	5/1893
D6	B4	0-4-0	10	81, 176, 95-103	10/1893
F6	T1	0-4-4T	10	1-10	4/1894
G6	G6	0-6-0T	10	257-266	6/1894
K6	A12	0-4-2	10	647-656	11/1894
R6	O2	0-4-4T	10	227-236	11/1894
S6	T1	0-4-4T	10	11-20	6/1895

Order No	Loco Class	Loco type	Number in class	Original running numbers	Date of completion of first loco
T6	T6	4-4-0	10	677-686	9/1895
X6	X6	4-4-0	10	657-686	12/1895
A7	T1	0-4-4T	10	358-367	6/1896
C7	G6	0-6-0T	4	267-270	11/1896
M7	M7	0-4-4T	25	242-256, 667-676	3/1897
T7	T7	4-2-2-0	1	720	8/1897
V7	M7	0-4-4T	10	31-40	3/1898
X7	G6	0-6-0T	5	271-275	12/1897
C8	C8	4-4-0	10	290-299	6/1898
D9	G6	0-6-0T	5	237-240, 279	9/1898
E9	M7	0-4-4T	10	22-26, 41-44, 241	1/1899
F9	F9	4-2-4T	1	773	4/1899
G9	T9	4-4-0	10	113-122	6/1899
K9	T9	4-4-0	5	280-284	10/1899
M9	G6	0-6-0T	5	160-162, 276-278	3/1900
O9	T9	4-4-0	5	285-289	1/1900
R9	G6	0-6-0T	5	348/9/51/3/4	5/1900
T9	T9	4-4-0	5	300-304	12/1900
X9	T9	4-4-0	5	305/7/10-12	2/1901
B10	M7	0-4-4T	5	112, 318-321	7/1900
C10	M7	0-4-4T	5	322-324, 356/7	8/1900
E10	E10	4-2-2-0	5	369-373	4/1901
G10	T9	4-4-0	5	313/4, 336-338	5/1901
K10	K10	4-4-0	5	329, 340-343	12/1901
L10	K10	4-4-0	5	344/5/7/93/4	12/1901
P10	K10	4-4-0	5	380-384	4/1902
S10	K10	4-4-0	5	385-389	5/1902
V10	K10	4-4-0	5	390-392, 135/6	6/1902
A11	K10	4-4-0	5	137-141	6/1902
C11	K10	4-4-0	5	142-146	9/1902
E11	K10	4-4-0	5	149-153	11/1902
G11	M7	0-4-4T	5	123/4/30	12/1902
H11	My	0-4-4T	5	374-378	2/1903
K11	Steam railcar (joint)	2	1,2 (joint with LBSCR)	4/1903	
L11	L11	4-4-0	5	154-158	5/1903
O11	L11	4-4-0	5	159/61/3/-5	5/1903
S11	S11	4-4-0	5	395-399	9/1903
V11	S11	4-4-0	5	400-404	6/1903
A12	A12	0-4-2	10	527-536	5/1887
B12	M7	0-4-4T	5	21/7-9,30	1/1904
C12	M7	0-4-4T	5	108-111, 379	3/1904
D12	L11	4-4-0	5	134,48,66-8	4/1904
F12	L11	4-4-0	5	169-173	8/1904
H12	Steam railcar	2	1,2	5/1904	
L12	L12	4-4-0	5	415-419	6/1904
O12	L12	4-4-0	5	420-424	9/1904
R12	L12	4-4-0	5	425-429	11/1904
T12	L12	4-4-0	5	430-434	2/1905
X12	M7	0-4-4T	5	104-107, 45	3/1905

Order No	Loco Class	Loco type	Number in class	Original running numbers	Date of completion of first loco
Y12	M7	0-4-4T	5	46-50	5/1905
B12	M7	0-4-4T	5	51-55	11/1905
D13	M7	0-4-4T	5	56-60	1/1906
F13	F13	4-6-0	5	330-334	4/1906
H13	Steam railcar	9	3-11	11/1905	
K13	L11	4-4-0	5	174/5, 407-409	5/1905
M13	L11	4-4-0	5	410-414	6/1906
P13	L11	4-4-0	5	405/6/35-7	9/1906
S13	L11	4-4-0	2	438-442	3/1907
A14	Steam railcar	2	12,13	5/1906	
B14	Steam railcar	2	14,15	6/1906	
C14	C14	2-2-0T	5	736-740	9/1906
D14	C14	2-2-0T	5	741-745	11/1906
E14	E14	4-6-0	1	335	12/1907
G14	G14	4-6-0	5	453-457	3/1908
K14	B4	0-4-0T	5	82-84, 746/7	4/1908

'M7' No 243, built at Nine Elms in 1897 as the second engine of the first batch of 25 of the class to Order Ref 'M7'.

Nine Elms Order Nos. 1910-1924

Order No	Loco Class	Loco type	Number in class	Original running numbers	Date of completion of first loco
P14	P14	4-6-0	5	448-452	10/1910
S14	S14	0-4-0T	2	101,147	9/1910
T14	T14	4-6-0	5	443-447	3/1911
X14	X14	0-4-4T	5	125-129	/1911
A15	X14	0-4-4T	5	131, 328, 479-81	/1911
B15	T14	4-6-0	5	458-462	12/1911
D15	D15	4-4-0	5	463-467	2/1912
G15	D15	4-4-0	5	468-472	9/1912
H15	H15	4-6-0	5	482/3/86-88	12/1913
K15	H15	4-6-0	5	484/5/9/90/1	4/1914
M15	H15	4-6-0	1	335	11/1914
N15	N15	4-6-0	5	736-740	9/1918
P15	N15	4-6-0	5	741-745	5/1919
S15	S15	4-6-0	5	497-501	3/1920
A16	S15	4-6-0	5	502-506	7/1920
C16	S15	4-6-0	5	507-511	11/1920
E16	S15	4-6-0	5	496, 512-515	2/1921
G16	G16	4-8-0T	4	492-495	7/1921
H16	H16	4-6-2T	5	516-520	11/1921
L16	N15	4-6-0	5	746-750	6/1922
N16	N15	4-6-0	5	751-755	11/1922
R16	H15	4-6-0	5	473-477	2/1924
T16	H15	4-6-0	5	478, 521-524	6/1924
A17	H15	4-6-0	5	330-334	10/1924

Eastleigh Order No G16 was also given as the class designation for the four massive 4-8-0T engines which entered service from July 1921 onwards. No 493 is seen here in later Southern livery and with clamps applied to the lower half of the smokebox door. Although no location is given it is likely the view was taken at its normal place of work, Feltham.

Two Accidents on Gomshall Bank

John Burgess

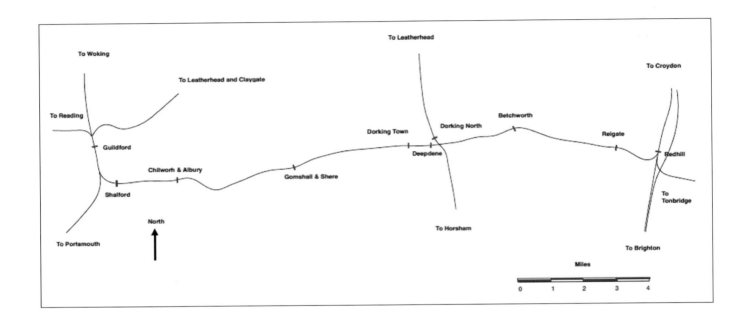

Route map Guildford to Redhill.

1: Chilworth 1892

If you have travelled between Guildford and Redhill on the former South Eastern Railway's Reading branch, just to the east of Chilworth Station on the down side of the line you may have noticed a box-tree topiary in the shape of a peacock perched on a chair, and wondered what this strange sculptured shrub is all about. Those in the know will be able to tell you that it is called Jessie's Seat, and that it is a memorial to a railway guard who lost his life in a railway accident which occurred on 29 February 1892.

A newspaper report in the *Surrey Advertiser* for 5 March 1892 describes the accident in some detail, but before doing so it may first be appropriate to undertake some brief scene-setting.

The line between Dorking and Guildford runs through some of the most beautiful scenery in Surrey, with the North Downs on the up side of the railway, and the Lower Greensand hills around Leith Hill on the down side. From the crossing of the River Mole near to Deepdene station, the line rises on a long ruling gradient of 1 in 96 to a summit at Welcome Bridge about a mile before the line reaches Gomshall and Shere station, before descending at the same ruling gradient (with a break of

about a mile shortly after Gomshall station where the line again rises at 1 in 100). The falling gradient continues through the next station at Chilworth and Albury, almost as far as Shalford.

The summit at Welcome Bridge is the highest point on the line, and in the days of steam was quite a challenge for the longer and heavier freight trains, although most passenger trains consisted of no more than four bogie coaches, and these trains barely tested the locomotives. The line also carried a great deal of freight traffic, indeed more than most lines in the South-East, that is until recent times.

On that leap year Monday night about 10pm, 29 February 1892, a long freight set off from Redhill consisting of 51 wagons hauled by two locomotives destined for Reading. The train was under the control of two guards, George White from Reading in the rear guard's van at the tail of the train, and Henry Hicks, also from Reading, in the front guard's van next to the second locomotive. Hicks had replaced another guard, who was absent on the day in question.

George White (the rear guard) gave evidence to the subsequent Inquest presided over by the Coroner. He stated that Henry Hicks was in charge of the train, and that they had checked the load before leaving Redhill. All couplings were properly connected and safety chains hooked up wherever possible. The load was within the allowed limit of 45 loaded wagons as 15 of the wagons were empty. The train was running at about 20 or 25 mph on the bank at Shere Heath (this is where the descent to the west of Gomshall is broken). White applied his brake as the train headed down towards Chilworth, and states that as he did so, the guard of a passing up train shouted to him but he did not understand what was meant.

Henry Forbes, driver of the train engine, confirmed the load of the train as 49 wagons and two brake vans. He later considered that the draw bar had broken as the train climbed over Shere Heath, but he did not notice anything until the collision.

Whatever, it is probable that a coupling broke and that the guard on the up train was trying to draw White's attention to this. As the locomotives slowed with a few attached wagons, the breakaway section gathered speed down the bank and collided with the front portion, smashing about 30 wagons across the tracks and down the embankment. The unfortunate Henry Hicks was thrown out of his van, and his lifeless body was discovered lying on the embankment. He was aged 52, and had worked for the SER for about 30 years.

The newspaper reported that a large breakdown gang arrived from Bricklayers Arms, and that single line working past the wreckage started on the following day, and by the Thursday the down line was also clear. The collision had broken the telegraph line, which also provided Post Office services between Guildford and Gomshall, Shere and Albury.

The Coroner recorded a verdict of accidental death, and recommended that means be devised to communicate between guards and drivers of freight trains. It was a valid point, although a vain hope as seventy years later, unfitted freights continued to run without any such aid, and it seems unlikely that the Coroner's suggestion would have helped in this case. Of course, where trains are fitted with automatic brakes, if a coupling fails, the brake is automatically applied on both sections of the train. With the benefit of hindsight, it is shameful that unfitted freights continued to be allowed to run for so many years after the availability of automatic brakes. This issue seemed to pass by the Coroner without mention, who would not in any event have had the specialist knowledge of the Railway Inspectorate.

In this case, there was also no Inquiry by the Board of Trade. Had there been one, a more perceptive investigation of the causes of the accident would have been carried out no doubt, with pertinent recommendations on working practices if considered necessary. Was this because the risk of working on the railway was considered to be an occupational hazard, and

Jessie's seat. *Christopher May*

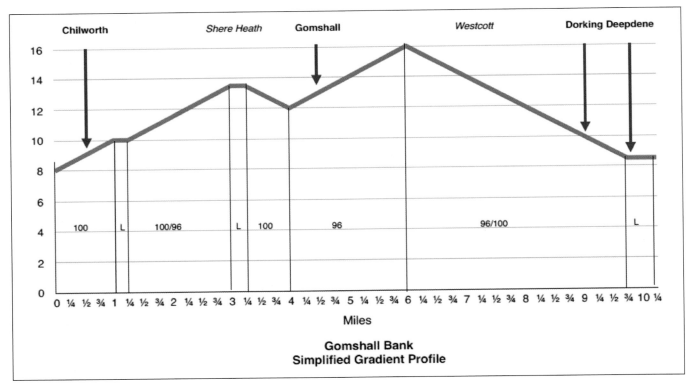

**Gomshall Bank
Simplified Gradient Profile**

Gradient profile.

lives of staff rated of less consequence than was the case with the lives of the travelling public? Certainly there does not appear to have been much real concern with what we would today call 'Health and Safety at work'. *(This very point about what was investigated and by whom has been touched on before in 'SW'. We can only repeat that it 'appears' most fatalities involving a passenger were investigated by the B of T but that incidents where there was no loss of life or just injuries/fatalities to railway staff appear to have come under the stewardship of the railway company. But again there were exceptions. If anyone can give a clear definition we would be grateful. Board of Trade accident reports are fairly easily accessed for most accidents but events investigated by the railways themselves appear either to have been largely forgotten or the files simply discarded and likely destroyed. Should anyone have a pile of such papers we would dearly love to see them – Ed.)*

The working of loose coupled freights took a great deal of skill and knowledge, requiring co-operation between the guard and the footplate crew. To avoid couplings being snatched, it was necessary to keep the train stretched out and the couplings taut while descending banks, which would require the rear guard to apply the brake as the train passed over the summit of the line, and on lengthy trains to stop at the summit and apply brakes on wagons within the train to check the tendency for the train to run away down the bank. Changes of grade from ascent to descent and back to ascent can lead to the couplings snatching, and the extreme forces so released can cause their failure, as more than likely happened here. As an aside, there are some graphic descriptions of loose freight working over the line between Ayr and Girvan, where heavy freights ran over a

switchback line with no less than six separate summits, told by the late David Smith in his books on the old Glasgow and South Western. If you can get hold of these writings, they are well worth a read. By contrast, Gomshall bank was chicken feed – and a long way from Ayrshire.

The topiary memorial remains to this day as a reminder of this accident. It is named Jessie's Seat after the guard's daughter in law, Jessie Wicks.

2: Gomshall 1904

Moving forward twelve years, a second serious accident occurred, this time at Gomshall and Shere station. On 20 February 1904, a special troop train left Gravesend at 8.25am bound for Southampton and carrying about 150 Northumberland Fusiliers. The train was routed via Redhill and Guildford with the troops due to sail to Mauritius. (The *Surrey Mirror* report stated the port of embarkation was Plymouth, but this is unlikely to have been the case.) At 10.20am at Gomshall, the train left the rails causing serious injuries, but fortunately with no fatalities. The locomotive ended up some 150 yards from the point at which the derailment took place, with severe damage to both the track and train.

The locomotive involved was described as a six coupled tender engine, No. 284, an 'O' class 0-6-0 in original condition with a dome-less boiler. It had recently had a heavy general repair and was in good working order. It was hauling a four-wheel brake van and six 6-wheeled coaches*.

An average then of 25 men per coach, although likely officers would have been more comfortably accommodated.

Debris from the 1892 accident.

On board the locomotive were Richard Paine, driver, and Frederick Leppard, fireman. The locomotive crew both lived in Redhill and had taken over the train from there. The guard was William Eldridge, who had been in charge of the train from Gravesend.

An Inquiry was held with the evidence centred around the speed of the train and the state of the permanent way. Bearing in mind that no speedometers were fitted to steam locomotives, working out the speed of the train was something of a detective job, and the Inspector, Major J W Pringle, was fortunate in being able to call for evidence from an assistant in the Engineering Department (Mr Messer) who had travelled over the line the previous day keeping a record of the speeds attained by the through train from Deal to Reading, with a passenger locomotive and three bogie coaches, which was considered to be comparable to the troop train. *(It would be interesting to know whether these speeds were recorded – Ed.)* In addition, the Inspector took evidence from the Permanent Way Inspector, William Corser, who reported on the state of the permanent way after the accident and the marks left by the derailment. Evidence was also given by staff on duty when the accident occurred, the guard, and the crew on the footplate.

Starting with the signalmen, Richard Baker at Dorking had recorded the troop train through Dorking at 10.12am, about three minutes ahead of its booked time. Frederick Nibley was on duty at Westcott signal cabin (an intermediate block post closed many years ago), and recorded the train as passing his signal box at 10.15am. Albert Smith at Gomshall stated that the train passed his box at 10.20am. He gave evidence that he thought the train was running at about 30 to 35 mph. He also noticed that it was 'running wide' of the down platform after it had passed his box, this being the very point at which it derailed and obstructed both lines – at which point he signalled 'obstruction' in both directions.

George Greer, Station Master at Gomshall, did not see the train pass, but stated that there were no speed restrictions through the station, although since the accident, a speed limit between Redhill and Reading of 40 mph for all trains had been introduced. Albert Chapman, relief signalman, was working in the goods yard and estimated that the train was running at 40 mph. Frederick Terry, goods checker, estimated that it was running at 35 to 40 mph.

William Eldridge, guard, stated that the train had passed Dorking at 10.11am. When they reached Gomshall, he estimated that the speed was 30 to 35 mph, and speed was rising from the top of the bank shortly before reaching Gomshall.

Richard Paine, driver, stated that the speed at the top of the bank would have been about 25 to 30 mph, and that he had run through Dorking at about 35 mph. Through Gomshall he considered that they were running at about 35 mph. The brake

Engine and tender of No 284 facing opposite directions – note the number and build plate from the tender, together with the vehicle body sheered off the underframe.

had not been applied between Dorking and Gomshall. Frederick Leppard, fireman, also thought that the speed was about 35 mph.

Evidence about the locomotive was taken from Mr J Welfare, Locomotive Inspector, and George Weston, Redhill Locomotive Foreman. The locomotive had returned to traffic after a heavy general repair on 24 December 1903, had been tried out on 25 December and returned to regular work on 26 December. Everything on the locomotive was in good order, and the wheels were true to gauge. (An interesting way to spend Christmas!)

Turning to the condition of the permanent way, evidence was taken from Mr P C Tempest, Chief Engineer, William Corser, Permanent Way Inspector, and others in the Permanent Way Department.

Mr Tempest advised that the rails had been turned in 1891. He had noticed that the first mark of the derailment was near to the trailing crossover opposite the up platform. The line through Gomshall was on a slight curve of 110 chains radius, ending just before the crossover. He considered that as laid, the line should have been good for running at up to 50 mph. He considered that having regard to the extent of the damage and the distance travelled after the derailment, the estimated speed of 35 mph given by the driver was considerably under

the mark. He had received reports of excessive speed on the line on 17 February and as a result had issued advice to keep speed below 50 mph, and he had appointed an Assistant to travel on the through train and record its speed. (This 'Assistant' who was supposedly travelling on the train is not mentioned further.)

William Corser, Permanent Way Inspector, advised that the rails had been laid in 1878, and subsequently turned. As laid, the rails were 82lbs/yard, reduced by wear to about 76/77lbs/yard. About one third of the chairs were 30lbs, the other two thirds being 45lbs. The sleepers had been checked the previous June and defective ones replaced. The line was laid on a mixture of Dungeness beach ballast and local sand, with more sand than ballast through Gomshall. He felt that the ballast was acceptable but not for speed in excess of 40 mph. There would be some liability for the line to slew at higher speeds.

William Worsfold, ganger, was not impressed with the sandy ballast, which he did not consider held the track sufficiently firmly. He had seen the troop train pass through the station, and estimated that it had been running at about 50 mph. Robert Jeffries, one of the gang working on the line, considered that the train was running at 40 to 50 mph.

Seen from the opposite side we see the front of the tender minus its front pair of wheels. The forces involved to effect some of the damage to the tender alone can only be imagined. Note the four-wheel hand trolley, which should not be seen as having had any bearing upon the accident. Gomshall and Shere station may just be glimpsed in the background. Interestingly, despite obvious damage to and distortion of the carriage side, there are no obvious broken windows.

Mr Messer reported on his findings travelling on the through train from Deal the day before the accident. He travelled in both directions over the line to Reading, measuring speed by observing the mileposts. In the down direction, the train had run through Dorking at 40 mph. By the summit, the speed had reduced to 18 mph. Once over the summit, speed increased rapidly and Messer had been unable to check the quarter mile posts, but he noted that the speed was the highest on the journey, exceeding the 57 mph he recorded running down Wellington College bank. He also noted that during the up journey of the through train on February 22 the train had passed through Gomshall at 52 mph, even though a 15 mph speed limit was in force at the time.

The Inspector applied himself to the evidence, including the conflicting views as to the speed of the troop train as it ran through the station. He had carried out an inspection of the accident site, and generally considered that the state of the track was quite adequate, but he too expressed misgivings about the condition of the ballast. Taking all the factors into account, he recommended that the track should be subject to a 50 mph speed restriction.

Turning to the question of the speed of the train, the Inspector applied some of his own detective work using the reported passing times provided by the signalmen recording the progress of the train. The eight minutes taken for the journey from Dorking to Gomshall of 4.75 miles suggest an average speed of 36 mph. Assuming that speed fell from 40 mph at Dorking to 25 mph at the summit, he calculated that the speed through Gomshall would have been in excess of 50 mph. He noted that Messer had recorded the actual speed of the timed train the previous day as lower at the summit, and higher through the station. He considered that, if necessary, the Company should give a longer period for trains to run through this section to avoid the need for excessive speed.

No 284 was badly damaged by the accident, but was taken into works, repaired and continued in service until it was withdrawn in 1911. It was one of the first batch of 'O' class locomotives, and was never rebuilt to run as class 'O1'.

The findings have some resonance with those of the Inquiry into the disaster at Sevenoaks after the derailment of a 'K' Class 2-6-4T in 1927, when the use of Dungeness ballast was reported to have contributed to the disaster, leading the Southern Railway to abandon its use and in future bring in all its ballast from the granite quarries at Meldon.

In this age, speedometers are universal, but not so in the days of the steam railway. Indeed much reliance was placed on the driver to judge his speed without the aid of this technology and many accidents occurred throughout the railway system because of a simple failure to keep to speed limits. The evidence from the various railwaymen also shows what variance in opinion there could be when judging speed. But even with the most modern aids, accidents do still occur as a result of excess speed, as recent incidents on the Croydon Tramlink have demonstrated.

From the ghost like images clearly there was work in progress here, railway men of several grades visible: reference the bowler hats present.

Spotting at Basingstoke and Worting Junction

Dave Clark, images and notes courtesy of The Transport Treasury

No 30765 *Sir Gareth* making its way west/south-west from Basingstoke with the ex-Wolverhampton service. The train consists of 10 coaches and appears to have almost every alternate vehicle different from its neighbour. In the background is the Eli Lilly building. (See the article 'Ambulance Trains at Basingstoke in WW2' by John Springer, commencing on page 82 of this issue.)

We make no excuses that this issue contains more than a small amount on the West of England main line (can one really have too much of a good thing?), exemplified here with a collection Robin Fell of the Transport Treasury (TT) pointed out to us under the above heading . Enthusiast Dave Clark – whose collection now resides with the TT – spent eight enjoyable hours at Basingstoke and then at Worting Junction on Saturday 8 September 1962 from 10.30am to 6.46pm both logging what he saw and photographing the same. Enjoy a day's nostalgia at the lineside.

Dave Clark spent the first part of the day up to around mid-day observing the comings and goings at Basingstoke shed. He makes particular mention of two engines, 'Schools' No 30925 and 'King Arthur' No 30765, both of which would cease work by the end of the year.

Next at 10.52am another 'Schools', No 30935, was observed on a Waterloo to Lymington through working, No 30935 being in charge as far as Brockenhurst. Shortly after at 11.03am No 30925 was ready at the station to take over the 8.54am ex-Waterloo. Whether this was a scheduled engine change is not reported, otherwise two hours from Waterloo to Basingstoke is somewhat excessive – we are not advised which engine was replaced. We are then told of 'Lord Nelson' No 30861 which was seen on an unreported 'up' working at 11.32am. (Likely there were numerous other special trains during the day as well.)

Next in the record of the day at 12.20pm comes 'N' No 31858 on a stopping service to Andover and Salisbury – possibly further. Taken from a similar vantage point to that of the last image, the lighting also shows up an area of the tender which appears to have been cleaned, although the remainder of the train and engine were left grimy. The first vehicle is of Maunsell origin followed by a Bulleid 3-set. On the extreme right is the remains of the Basingstoke – Alton line then leading only as far as the Thornycroft Works.

Dave Clark then reports No 30765 moving off shed and changing engines to be ready to depart with the 12.12pm ex-Wolverhampton service which it will work through to Bournemouth.

We now miss one train, which was the 12.30pm departure from Basingstoke to Weymouth (11.22 am ex-Waterloo) hauled by another 'Schools' No 30934 and instead we are treated to a 'Lord Nelson' No 30857 on a through working to Bradford, due to depart Basingstoke at 12.38pm.

No 30857 *Lord Howe* **passing the up sidings at Basingstoke shortly before entering the station. This inter-regional service is formed of 11 vehicles, a mixture of LMR and ER stock. The 'A' class headcode signifying an 'express' type working was used on all regions except the Southern where 'route' codes were used instead. The exception was the inter-regional workings as seen here. Note also the difference in levels between the sidings and the running lines, the former laid on the level and the main lines falling slightly from Worting in the direction of the station.**

We must now imagine Dave Clark walking along the cess westwards to where he next started to point his camera at Worting Junction – was he perhaps challenged by the signalman here and asked to show his lineside permit? (Such things could be obtained upon application [was there a fee?] and would allow the holder to walk the line 'at own risk' of course, between specific points.) Consequently there is a gap of over an hour before the next train is recorded, 'S15' No 30826 coming off the West of England line at Worting Junction whilst above an unidentified service from the Bournemouth line passes over on Battledown flyover.

No 30826 on an up local from Salisbury leaning to the curve, having just passed under the flyover. To the left, the Bournemouth line runs south towards Micheldever and Winchester. In the 'V' of the junction between the two down lines had once been where the signal box (controlling what was originally a flat junction) had been located. This was closed in 1897. The train is another Bulleid 3-set with a 4-wheel van attached to the rear, the light load of little consequence to an engine of this type.

No 30839 leaning to the curve with the 2.43pm service to Salisbury. Unusually perhaps, Dave Clark did not record any BR 'Standard' classes on passenger workings although the various 73xxx, 75xxx and even 76xxx tender engine classes were certainly active on such trains in this period. Indeed some spotters regarded such engines as somehow of less interest than the home grown product. This of course was the observers' perspective, most crews just happy to have a good and capable machine regardless of its origins. No 30839 certainly appears to have a reasonable train attached to the (flat-sided) tender and whilst not having the speed capabilities of a 'Pacific' or 73xxx, the 'S15' could certainly progress well, although if pushed the ride might well turn out to be somewhat rough.

The rest of the photographic day was spent in the vicinity of the junction and where eight different trains were recorded. The first of these being another local hauled by an 'S15', this time No 30839.

Crossing over the down Bournemouth line, we now see No 34103 *Calstock* with the 2.43pm inter-regional terminating at Southampton Central. (With duty numbers a-plenty in evidence on several of the engines depicted, it would be very useful if we had the summer 1962 loco workings to hand!) From the slight movement blur it is clear the engine was working hard but perhaps also a few minutes behind time – judging by the 'S15' having been seen first and no sign of this service in the background. No 34103 would survive until the end of the summer of 1965.

12

SATURDAY, 8th SEPTEMBER

No. 40—Party Traffic—continued

Name	No. of Passengers		From	To	Train	Station to Reserve
	1st	2nd				
St. Marks Sunday School	—	100	Hinton Admiral	Weymouth	9.49 am	Eastleigh (8.40 am)
Bitterne Park Baptist Church	—	36	St. Denys	Christchurch	9.53 am changing at So'ton Cen. into 10.22 am	St. Denys assist.
Mr. Maynes	—	8	Bournemouth Cen.	Waterloo	10.0 am	Bournemouth West (9†38 am) one comp.
Bournemouth and Boscombe F.C.	—	16	Bournemouth Cen.	Waterloo	10.22 am	Swanage (9.20 am) near dining car.
Shirley Oaks	—	26	Weymouth	Waterloo	11.2 am	Weymouth
Mr. Potter	6	—	Bournemouth Cen.	Waterloo	11.13 am	Bournemouth West (11.0 am) one First class smoking compartment
P. & O. Line	6	—	Southampton Cen.	Waterloo	1.20 pm	Weymouth (11.25 am) one First class compartment near dining car
Invalid Mrs. Brown and escorts	—	3	Swanage NON-INFECTIOUS RECUMBENT PATIENT	Woking	1.23 pm	Swanage—one compartment for exclusive use.
A.T.C. (1460 Squadron)	3	28	Portsmouth & S'sea (ex Chichester)	Banbury	1.33 pm	Portsmouth Hbr. (1.28 pm)
2nd Rayners Lane Scouts	—	19	Lymington Pier	Waterloo	3.30 pm	Lymington Pier.
Whitehall Hill A.V. Club	—	10	Bournemouth Cen.	Waterloo	5.18 pm	Bournemouth West (4.55 pm).
Bitterne Park Baptist Church	—	36	Christchurch	St. Denys	5.53 pm changing at So'ton Cen. into 6.49 pm	Bournemouth West (5†13 pm). So'ton Cen. assist.
A.T.C. (2258 Squadron)	4	27	Brockenhurst (ex Waterloo)	West Moors	6.6 pm	Brockenhurst
St. Marks Sunday School	—	100	Weymouth	Hinton Admiral (Special Stop)	6.30 pm	Weymouth.
St. Lawrence Church Youth Club	—	24	Salisbury	Downton	8.30 pm	Salisbury.
Moordown Youth Fellowship	—	24	Lymington Pier	Bournemouth Cen.	8.35 pm changing at Brockenhurst into 8.53 pm	Lymington Pier. Eastleigh (7.22 pm).

Having access to the Special Traffic Notices for the day in question we had hoped it might be possible to identify some of the more interesting movements seen on that day. Unfortunately and despite much effort, this has just not proved possible and so as compensation a page detailing some of the 'Party Traffic' – many of whom would have been on trains seen in these images – is included.

Spotting in steam days could also provide the occasional unexpected visitor as well...

Possibly the most unusual working of the day came at 4.03pm when former LBSCR 'K' No 32345 rounded the curve from the Salisbury direction. Other than recording the time, we have no idea regarding the working. The leading vehicle is without doubt a Bulleid design coach once forming part of set No 981, although seen here disbanded and instead part of a loose formation.

The 'K' was shortly followed from the same direction by No 34020 *Seaton* in grimy work-a-day condition. It is shown carrying a No '9' duty board, which relates to a Nine Elms turn. Notice in the background the 3H 'Hampshire' unit climbing the last stage of the 1 in 106 gradient on to the flyover, likely a Southampton to Reading service.

A short 'stretch of the legs' slightly further south to where a foot crossing dissects the Bournemouth line and the chance to record 'Lord Nelson' No 30857 *Lord Howe* again, this time on its return working south at 4.40pm. The headcode indicates this is another inter-regional train, which the Eastleigh-based engine has probably taken over at Oxford. As with the members of the 'Schools' class, this was the last year the type was active and all had ceased work by the end of 1962. (Dave Clark also recorded a GWR 'Hall', No 7900, at the same spot half an hour later – but we felt it best not to include it!)

Above: **For the penultimate view we have yet another inter-regional train with No 30765 *Sir Gareth* heading north this time and possibly preparing for an engine change at Basingstoke. (Certain services/times of year dictated how far the Southern Region would work: Basingstoke, Reading, Oxford or on occasions even Banbury.) Due to their variety, the vehicles behind the tender *could* be the same as those on the down train earlier in the day, although this time it will be noted the up train only has nine vehicles compared with ten on the down. Dave Clark recorded the time as 5.50pm.**

Opposite: **And for the final view in this sequence (although more examples from the various Transport Treasury archives will appear in the next issue) we have walked the two miles back to Basingstoke where '9F' No 92212 leads a train of empty tank-cars en route to Fawley. The '9F' will come off at Eastleigh to be replaced by a pair of tank engines for the final few miles through Southampton and on to the branch. Sometimes referred to as 'space-ships' by the Eastleigh crews, these engines were certainly masters of the job, although when worked hard they needed a fireman prepared to do likewise. On weekdays, the trains were routed south from Didcot via Newbury and Winchester Chesil but unless there was good reason, the cross-country route was not available after about 9.00am on Saturday and all day Sunday. Dave Clark has taken the view by standing on the remains of the Basingstoke & Alton line, which since the 1930s had been truncated at Thorneycroft's siding but was still in occasional use at the time. Ironically the same track still survives at the time of writing but has not seen any rail movement for many years. The story goes that back in the 1980s, an adventurous diesel driver decided to see how far he might get towards Alton but sense prevailed and he decided not to pursue his ambition much beyond where we are standing. Again the Eli Lilly building is in the background, whilst the buffer stop on the left marks the western limit of the down goods yard and close to where wounded soldiers were unloaded in WW2 – again refer to the John Springer article.**

All images copyright The Transport Treasury

Salisbury to Exeter Part 2

Jeffery Grayer

'Thirty years of change – Infrastructure and train services'

In this, the second article of the series, Jeffery Grayer recalls the changes made following the Western Region takeover of the former SR main line west of Wilton in 1963. These changes were embodied in the closure of a number of the smaller stations; the closure of branch lines and associated junctions; the re-routing of most freight traffic; the substitution of steam operated express and local stopping services with a diesel semi-fast service and, perhaps most significantly of all for the long term future of the line, singling of large parts of the route. Future articles will look at the changes in motive power that the route has seen over the years and the changes in signalling from a manually fully signalled main line to a semi-automated secondary route.

Although many commentators over the years have considered that the rot set in with the boundary changes of 1963, which saw the Salisbury – Exeter trunk route west of Wilton transferred from the Southern Region to the Western Region, this tends to overlook the fact that had the line

remained within the gambit of the SR then surely similar economies and retrenchment would have had to take place given the financial situation and thinking of the time. Hindsight is a wonderful thing and who could have foreseen in those dark days of declining rail usage of the 1960s the surge in passenger numbers which has occurred since privatisation. This short sighted emasculation of a former main line has, only in recent years, been partly redressed and this too at significant cost.

Reduced to its basic form, this view of the west end of the former Seaton Junction station reveals the pared down nature of this former main line. Where once a double track with passing loops graced an interchange for the branch to Seaton, just a single line now serves the semi-fast diesel service seen here with a 'Class 50' in charge of a Waterloo train passing non-stop through the closed station. The former up loop and a siding were retained to serve the adjacent dairy facility but by the time of this view the latter had closed as witnessed by the rusting rails. The now empty nameboard on the former up platform and the grassy track bed of the former Seaton branch seen on the far left epitomise the drastically changed fortunes of this location and of the line in general.

In 1963 two main lines from the capital serving Exeter and the West were considered something of a luxury and given that the WR route to Paddington accounted for some 80 percent of the passenger traffic between the Devon city and the metropolis it was only logical that the SR route would be relegated to secondary status. At the time of the WR takeover, the railway was not even covering its operational costs and it could certainly no longer support multi-portioned summer holiday steam powered trains to a wide variety of West Country destinations. In fact the SR lines west of Salisbury as early as 1957 were apparently failing to cover even their direct costs by as much as £800k p.a.

RATIONALE

To address the need for drastic cost reductions, the WR plan was to close the smaller unprofitable stations and junctions together with their associated branch lines, operate a semi-fast diesel hauled service and with the remaining stations spaced out strategically along the route to act as railheads for the surrounding areas; also to remove freight and local passenger services thus freeing up capacity and so enable large portions of this double track main line to be reduced to single track with passing loops.

TIMETABLE CHANGES

The 7 September 1964 thus saw the start of a new era of semi-fast rather than express services on the line. With one exception, the 01:10 newspaper train with through coaches for Plymouth, services from Waterloo ceased to run beyond Exeter St. Davids. Now just five semi-fast services at two hourly intervals operated, with the traditional 'ACE' slot of an 11:00 departure from Waterloo now a semi-fast from Waterloo terminating at Salisbury where passengers had to change into a retimed Brighton – Plymouth service. Not surprisingly, overcrowding west from Salisbury was often the order of the day under this

arrangement. For the present, the few remaining local services west of Salisbury continued to operate, generally with DMUs, pending closure of many of the intermediate stations. The weekday timetable for the period from September 1964 until June 1965 is shown pages 32-35.

From this it can be seen that the down stopping trains were generally timetabled to leave Salisbury shortly after the semi-fast service had left. Also, for the moment there continued to be some stopping services continuing west of Exeter operated by DMUs to both Plymouth and to Ilfracombe and of course the long standing through service from Brighton to Plymouth continued to run via Okehampton until it too was cut back to Exeter in March 1967.

BRANCH LINE & STATION CLOSURES

Prior to the WR takeover, the small station of Sutton Bingham had closed on the last day of 1962 but this was nothing compared to the publication of the Beeching Report in March 1963, which foretold that the branch lines to Lyme Regis, Seaton, Sidmouth and Exmouth were all to be included in the closure proposals. Of these, Lyme Regis was the first to go, closing on 29 November 1965, followed by Seaton on 7 March 1966. Finally the Sidmouth branch and the line to Exmouth via Tipton St Johns closed from 6 March 1967.

The railway from Exeter to Exmouth however was to stave off closure and is still very much with us, enjoying a half-hourly service for much of the day.

Overshadowed by the closure of the ever popular Somerset & Dorset line on the same day, 6 March 1966, the withdrawal of passenger services from a number of the smaller stations on

Using the former 'up' line, a maroon liveried 'Warship'-hauled Exeter service rolls into the passing loop at Gillingham, the severance of the former down line is clearly visible just before the overbridge. As the main station buildings were also situated on the up side, all services were routed to this platform wherever operationally possible.

Table 2 — Weekdays

London Waterloo and Salisbury to Exeter

Station		MX	A		E	H	B		C		H	C	H	✕ D	E		⊗ G	E
LONDON WATERLOO	d	..	1 10	..	..	..	..	..	..	..	..	..	..	9 00	..	..	11 00	..
WOKING	d	..	..	..	..	..	..	..	..	..	..	..	..	9 29	..	..	11 29	..
BASINGSTOKE	d	..	..	..	..	..	..	..	..	..	..	..	..	9 56	..	..	11 56	..
ANDOVER JUNCTION	d	..	2 29	..	..	..	..	..	..	..	..	..	..	10 18	..	..	12 18	..
SALISBURY	d	2 40	3 00	..	3 25	..	..	..	..	..	..	8 10	..	10 44	10 50	..	13 04	13 10
WILTON SOUTH	d	..	..	..	..	..	..	..	..	..	..	8 16	..	10 56	..	..	..	13 16
DINTON	d	..	..	..	..	..	..	..	..	..	..	8 24	..	11 04	..	..	..	13 24
TISBURY	d	..	..	..	3 45	..	..	..	..	..	..	8 32	..	11 12	..	..	..	13 32
SEMLEY	d	..	..	..	3 55	..	..	..	..	..	..	8 40	..	11 20	..	..	..	13 40
GILLINGHAM	d	..	..	..	4 09	..	..	..	..	..	..	8 46	..	11 28	..	..	13 30	13 46
TEMPLECOMBE	d	3b45	..	..	4 25	..	..	..	7 05	..	..	8 56	..	11 10	11 22	..	13 42	13 56
MILBORNE PORT HALT	d	..	..	..	..	..	..	..	7 12	..	..	9 01	..	11 43	..	..	..	14 01
SHERBORNE	d	4 00	..	..	4 41	..	..	..	7 20	..	..	9 08	..	11 32	11 50	..	13 52	14 08
YEOVIL JUNCTION	a	4 08	..	..	4 49	..	..	..	7 27	..	..	9 15	..	11 41	11 57	..	14 01	14 15
61 YEOVIL TOWN	a	4 20	..	..	5 06	..	..	..	7 35	..	..	9 24	..	11 48	12 05	..	14 08	14 23
	d	..	..	..	..	..	..	..	6 25	..	7 50	9 06	..	11 33	11 52	..	13 53	14 11
YEOVIL JUNCTION	d	..	..	..	..	..	..	..	6 33	..	8 00	9 16	..	11 42	11 58	..	14 02	14 17
CREWKERNE	d	..	..	..	..	..	..	..	6 49	..	8 14	9 29	..	..	12 11	..	..	14 29
CHARD JUNCTION	d	..	..	..	..	..	..	..	7 03	..	8 26	9 41	..	..	12 23	..	..	14 41
AXMINSTER	a	..	..	..	..	..	..	..	7 10	..	8 33	9 48	..	12 04	12 30	..	14 24	14 48
66 LYME REGIS	a	..	..	..	..	..	..	..	7 33	..	..	10 10	..	..	13 24	..	15 13	15 13
	d	..	..	..	..	..	..	..	6h31	7 38	..	9 25	..	11 42	13 30	..	..	..
AXMINSTER	d	..	..	..	..	..	..	..	7 13	8 00	8 36	9 48	..	12 05	12 30	..	13 52 14 25	14 48
SEATON JUNCTION	a	..	..	..	..	..	..	..	7 18	8 05	8 41	9 54	..	12 13	12 36	..	13 58	14 54
67 SEATON	a	..	..	..	..	..	..	..	7 44	8 20	8 55	10 07	..	12 48	12 48	..	14 13	15 10
	d	..	..	..	..	..	..	..	6k10	7 50	8 26	9 38	..	11 58	11 58	..	13 40	14 35
SEATON JUNCTION	d	..	..	..	..	..	..	..	7 21	8 06	8 43	9 54	..	12 14	12 36	..	13 59	14 54
HONITON	d	..	..	..	..	..	..	..	7 36	8 19	8 57	10 07	..	12 49	..	..	14 15	15 07
SIDMOUTH JUNCTION	a	..	..	..	..	..	..	..	7 42	8 25	9 03	10 13	..	12 30	12 55	..	14 22 14 45	15 13
68 SIDMOUTH	a	..	..	..	..	..	..	..	8 27	8 52	9 28	10 40	..	13 07	14 07	..	15 13	15 13
68 BUDLEIGH SALTERTON	a	..	..	..	..	..	..	..	..	9 00	..	10 54	..	..	..	..	15 20	15 20
68 SIDMOUTH	d	..	..	..	..	..	..	..	7 15	..	8 35	9 45	..	11 45	12 20	..	14 13	14 13
SIDMOUTH JUNCTION	d	..	..	..	..	..	..	..	7 47	8 26	9 05	10 14	..	12 31	12 56	..	14 23 14 46	15 14
WHIMPLE	d	..	..	..	..	..	..	..	7 53	8 31	9 11	10 20	..	13 02	..	..	14 29	15 20
BROAD CLYST	d	..	..	..	..	..	..	..	7 59	8 36	9 17	10 25	..	13 08	..	..	14 36	15 25
PINHOE	d	..	..	..	..	..	..	..	8 04	8 41	9 22	10 30	..	13 13	..	..	14 41	15 30
ST. JAMES' PARK HALT	d	..	..	..	..	..	..	..	8 10	8 47	..	..	..	..	..	..	14g47	..
EXETER CENTRAL	a	4 57	..	..	..	..	..	..	8 12	8 50	9 29	10 37	..	12 48	13 20	..	14 49 15 02	15 37
69 EXMOUTH	a	6 33	..	..	..	..	..	..	8 41 c	..	10 38	11 39	..	13 39	14 13	..	15 39 15 39	16 25
EXETER CENTRAL	d	5 10	5 20	..	7 10	8 09	8 55	..	9 42	10 42	11 40	12 51	13 19	13 26	..	..	15 05	15 39
EXETER ST. DAVID'S	a	5 14	5 24	..	7 13	8 12	8 58	..	9 45	10 45	11 43	12 55	13 22	13 31	..	..	15 09	15 42

Heavy figures indicate through carriages
For general notes see page 49

For the train service between Exeter St. David's and North Devon and North Cornwall see Tables 59 and 73

For other trains between St. James' Park Halt and Exeter see Table 69

For the principal train service between London and Exeter see Table 1

A Through train to Plymouth (via Okehampton). Connection for Ifracombe dep. Exeter Central 5.06 (See Table 59).
B Through train from Exmouth (dep. 7.44) to Ilfracombe (arr. 10.15).
C Through train to Plymouth (via Okehampton)
D Through train to Okehampton (arr 14.01) and Padstow (arr. 16.10).
E Through train to Ilfracombe
G Through train and ⊗ from Brighton (dep. 10.25) to Plymouth (via Okehampton)
H Through train from Exmouth

b Arr. 3.17
c Arr. 9.13 from Sidmouth Junction and beyond via Tipton St. John's
g Saturdays only
h 🚌 (Southern National) from Lyme Regis (Langford's Shop)
k 🚌 (Southern or Western National) from Seaton (Sea Front) to Axminster (Square)

---

the Salisbury – Exeter route went largely unrecorded in the same month. The nine stations closed were Wilton South, Dinton, Semley, Templecombe, Milborne Port, Chard Junction, Seaton Junction, Broad Clyst and Pinhoe. As previously mentioned, the same day had seen the end of the branch to Seaton. It had been the intention to close Sidmouth Junction station at the same time but the closure of the Sidmouth/Exmouth via Tipton St. Johns branch took another year to achieve. Both Tisbury and Whimple were also candidates for closure but they were reprieved and remain open today. The redoubtable Gerry Fiennes, the WR General Manager and never one to mince his words, felt that the clamour by locals and MPs to retain stations such as Tisbury, Templecombe and Yeovil Junction meant that, "…they have got what they deserved: an express service far slower than before and to my belief uncompetitive with road," i.e. the A303 which was due to be upgraded. Half a century later we are still waiting for it, although improved in parts, the A303 remains notoriously slow even today, particularly the long stretch of single carriageway through the Blackdown Hills east of Honiton and of course the single carriageway north of Salisbury skirting Stonehenge. (DO NOT try to use the A303 westbound from late morning on any Friday from Spring to Autumn and almost every Sunday or Bank Holiday evening in the return direction! Your editor speaks from bitter experience.)

Table 2

Weekdays

London Waterloo and Salisbury to Exeter

		E		H	C			E	A			⌖	SX					✕	
			✕			✕												✕	
LONDON WATERLOO	d	..	13 00	..	..	15 00	..	..	..	..	..	17 00	..	18 00	..	..	..	19 00	..
WOKING	d	..	13 29	..	..	15 29	..	..	..	..	..	17 29	..	18 29	..	..	..	19 29	..
BASINGSTOKE	d	..	13 56	..	..	15 56	..	..	..	..	..	17 56	..	18 56	..	..	..	19 56	..
ANDOVER JUNCTION	d	..	14 18	..	..	16 18	..	..	..	..	..	18 28	..	19 18	..	..	..	20 18	..
SALISBURY	d	..	14 44	..	14 55	16 44	..	..	17 25	..	..	18 54	..	19a44	..	19 55	..	20 44	..
WILTON SOUTH	d	..	..	..	15 01	..	..	..	17 31	..	..	..	..	..	..	20 01	..	..	..
DINTON	d	..	..	..	15 09	..	..	..	17 39	..	..	..	..	..	..	20 09	..	..	..
TISBURY	d	..	..	..	15 17	..	..	..	17 46	..	..	19 12	..	..	..	20 16	..	..	..
SEMLEY	d	..	..	..	15 25	..	..	..	17 54	..	..	19 20	..	..	..	20 21	..	..	..
GILLINGHAM	d	..	15 10	..	15 31	17 10	..	..	18 00	..	..	19 27	..	..	..	20 27	..	21 10	..
TEMPLECOMBE	d	..	15 22	..	15 42	17 22	..	..	18 10	..	..	19 39	..	..	..	20 31	..	..	..
MILBORNE PORT HALT	d	..	..	..	15 47	..	..	..	18 15	..	..	19 46	..	..	..	20 37	..	..	..
SHERBORNE	d	..	..	..	15 54	17 32	17 42	..	18 22	..	..	19 53	..	..	..	20 43	..	21 27	..
YEOVIL JUNCTION	a	..	15 35	..	16 01	..	17 51	..	18 29	..	..	20 02	..	..	..	20 53	..	21 36	..
61 YEOVIL TOWN	a	..	15 45	..	16 07	..	..	18 00	..	18 38	..	..	20 10	..	..	..	21 02	..	21 45	..
	d	..	15 28	..	15 55	..	..	..	..	18 23	..	..	19 55	..	..	..	..	..	21 30	..
YEOVIL JUNCTION	d	..	15 36	..	16 03	..	..	..	18 31	..	..	20 03	..	..	..	..	..	21 37	..
CREWKERNE	d	..	..	..	16 15	..	17 49	..	18 44	..	..	20 17	..	..	..	..	..	21 51	..
CHARD JUNCTION	d	..	..	..	16 27	..	..	..	18 56	..	..	..	..	..	..	..	..	..	..
AXMINSTER	a	..	15 58	..	16 34	..	18 03	..	19 03	..	..	20 31	..	..	..	..	..	22 05	..
66 LYME REGIS	a	..	16 23	..	..	..	18 26	..	19 23	..	..	21g02	..	..	..	..	..	22g37	..
	d	..	15 35	..	..	..	17 15	..	18 30	..	19 27	19h46	..	..	..	..	..	..	..
AXMINSTER	d	..	15 59	..	16 35	..	18 04	..	19 04	..	19 53	20 32	..	..	..	..	..	22 06	..
SEATON JUNCTION	a	..	..	..	16 40	..	..	..	19 09	..	19 59	20 40	..	..	..	..	..	..	..
67 SEATON	a	..	..	..	16 55	..	..	..	19 22	..	..	21g10	..	..	..	..	..	22p40	..
	d	..	..	..	16 25	..	..	..	18 55	..	19 25	19t45	..	..	..	..	..	21y25	..
SEATON JUNCTION	d	..	..	..	16 41	..	..	..	19 10	..	20 05	20 41	..	..	..	..	..	..	..
HONITON	d	..	..	..	16 54	..	..	18 55	19 23	..	20 23	20 55	..	..	..	..	..	22 22	..
SIDMOUTH JUNCTION	d	..	16 19	..	17 00	..	18 24	19 01	19 29	..	20 30	21 03	..	..	..	..	..	22f35	..
68 SIDMOUTH	a	..	16 50	..	17 40	19 00	..	..	..	..	..	..	..	..	..	..	..	22f57	..
68 BUDLEIGH SALTERTON	a	..	16 57	..	18 04	19 07	..	..	..	..	..	..	..	..	..	..	..	23f02	..
68 SIDMOUTH	d	15 40	..	..	..	17 44	..	..	..	19 53	..	..	..	..	..	..	..	..	..
SIDMOUTH JUNCTION	d	16 02	..	16 20	17 01	18 25	..	19 01	19 30	..	20 35	21 04	..	..	..	..	..	22f36	..
WHIMPLE	d	16 08	..	..	17 08	..	..	19 07	19 36	..	20 42	..	..	..	..	..	..	..	..
BROAD CLYST	d	16 14	..	..	17 13	..	..	19 13	19 42	..	20 48	..	..	..	..	..	..	..	..
PINHOE	d	16 19	..	..	17 18	..	..	19 17	19 46	..	20 53	..	..	..	..	..	..	..	..
ST. JAMES' PARK HALT	d	..	..	..	17 24	..	..	..	..	..	..	..	..	..	..	..	..	..	..
EXETER CENTRAL	a	16 26	..	16 35	17 26	..	18 40	19 24	19 53	..	21 00	21 19	..	..	..	..	..	22 48	..
69 EXMOUTH	a	17 03	..	17 03	..	18 02	..	19 15	..	..	20 45	21 44	..	21 44	..	..	..	23 20	..
EXETER CENTRAL	d	16 30	..	16 38	17 18	17 45	18 43	..	19 30	..	19 58	21 26	..	..	..	..	..	22 51	..
EXETER ST. DAVID'S	a	16 33	..	16 42	17 18	17 48	18 47	..	19 33	..	20 01	21 30	..	..	..	..	..	22 55	..

Heavy figures indicate through carriages
For general notes see page 49

For the train service between Exeter St. David's
and North Devon and North Cornwall see
Tables 59 and 73

For other trains between St. James' Park Halt
and Exeter see Table 69

For the principal train service between London
and Exeter see Table 1

A Through train to Barnstaple Junction (arr. 21.19)
C Through train to Plymouth (via Okehampton)
E Through train to Ilfracombe
H Through train from Exmouth (dep. 16.40) to
   Ilfracombe (arr. 19.10)

f Fridays only
g 🚌 (Southern National) from Axminster
h 🚌 (Southern National) from Lyme Regis
   (Langford's Shop)
p 🚌 (Southern or Western National) from
   Axminster Station to Seaton (Sea Front); on
   Wednesdays and Saturdays arr. Seaton (Sea
   Front) 23.47
t 🚌 (Southern or Western National) from
   Seaton (Sea Front) to Axminster Square
y 🚌 (Southern National) from Seaton (Sea Front)
   to Axminster Square. Not on Wednesdays and
   Saturdays.

SINGLING

The Salisbury to Exeter route was destined to become the English prototype for secondary main line singling and simplification as detailed in Beeching's Trunk Route Rationalisation document published in 1965. Other routes that would be in line for similar treatment on the WR were Swindon – Gloucester, Princes Risborough – Aynho Junction, Oxford – Worcester, and Castle Cary – Dorchester (and for a time the Berks and Hants between Westbury and Taunton). Given the public clamour resulting from these proposals, the then British Railways Board Chairman Sir Stanley Raymond had to be drafted in to appear on local West Country television to deny rumours of complete closure of the Salisbury – Exeter route which were rife at the time.

Instead the first phase of route singling got underway on 2 April 1967 when the 26 mile section from Wilton South to Templecombe was tackled. Crossing facilities were retained at Gillingham whilst only the former up platform at Tisbury was utilised. Double track was retained for the six miles between Templecombe and Sherborne but it was planned that the fifty odd miles thence to Pinhoe were to see crossing loops only at the now closed Chard Junction and at Honiton. Rather than

Table 2   **Weekdays**

Exeter to Salisbury and London Waterloo

Station				🍴	✕			A	J	E	C	H	✕ K	D	H		G ⊗
EXETER ST. DAVID'S .. .. d					7 20			8 11	8 34	8 51	9·48	10 10	10 30	11 45	11 59	12 10	12 25
EXETER CENTRAL .... a					7 23			8 14	8 37	8 54	9 51	10 13	10 33	11 48	12 02	12 13	12 28
69 EXMOUTH .. .. .. d			6 40	6 40	7 15						9 15		10 00	11 15			12 00
EXETER CENTRAL .... d	6 20		6 25	6 45	7 25	7 35	8 00				9 54		10 35	11 50			12 30
ST. JAMES' PARK HALT .. d						7 37	8 02				9 59			11 55			
PINHOE .... d				6 50		7 43	8 08				10 04			12 00			
BROAD CLYST .. .. d				6 55		7 47	8 12				10 11			12 07			
WHIMPLE .. .. d				7 02		7 55	8 19				10 18						
SIDMOUTH JUNCTION .. a	6 42			7 09	7 38	8 02	8 26				10 48			12 14			12 43
68 SIDMOUTH .... a	7 08				8 27	8 27	8 52				10 40		11 13				13 07
68 BUDLEIGH SALTERTON .. d				7 07							9 45		10 10				12 20
68 SIDMOUTH .... d				7 15									10 23	11 45			
SIDMOUTH JUNCTION .. d				7 10	7 39		8 35				10 18		10 49	12 15			12 44
HONITON .... d			6 38	7 20	7 48		8 43				10 27						12 24
SEATON JUNCTION .. a				7 29							10 36						12 33
67 SEATON .... a				7 44							10 55						12 48
SEATON .... d			6h10		7h15						10 20		11 58				
SEATON JUNCTION .. d				7 33							10 37						12 34
AXMINSTER .. .. a			6 49	7 38	7 59						10 42		11 06	12 39			13 01
66 LYME REGIS .... a			7 33		8 26						11 28		11 28	13 24			13 24
LYME REGIS .... d			7 38								9 25		10 45	11 42			12 40
AXMINSTER .. .. d			6 50		8 00						10 43		11 07	12 40			13 02
CHARD JUNCTION .. d			7 00								10 51			12 48			
CREWKERNE .... d			7 12		8 18						11 02		11 25	13 00			13 20
YEOVIL JUNCTION .. a			7 22		8 28						11 12			13 10			13 30
61 YEOVIL TOWN .... a			7 35		8 37						11 20			13 16			13 40
YEOVIL TOWN .... d	6 42	7 15	7 30		8 20						11 05			13 00			13 24
YEOVIL JUNCTION .. d	6 51	7 23	7 41		8 29						11 14			13 12			13 31
SHERBORNE .... d	6 59	7 33	7 49		8 39						11 22		11 39	13 20			13 41
MILBORNE PORT HALT .. d	7 06		7 57								11 29			13 27			
TEMPLECOMBE .. .. d	7 11		8 02								11 35		11 50	13 33			
GILLINGHAM .... d	7 20	7 49	8 12		8 50						11 45		12 02	13 43			13 59
SEMLEY .. .. d	7 28		8 20		9 02						11 53			13 51			
TISBURY .... d	7 35	8 04	8 28								12 00			13 59			
DINTON .. .. d	7 41		8 35								12 06			14 06			
WILTON SOUTH .... d	7 50		8 43								12 14			14 14			
SALISBURY .. .. a	7 55	8 23	8 49		9 30						12 20		12 30			14 20	14 27
ANDOVER JUNCTION .. a			9 34		9 58						12 57					14 59	14 59
BASINGSTOKE .. .. a		9 10	10 09		10 20						13 20					15 20	15 20
WOKING .. .. a			10 46								13 46					15 47	15 47
LONDON WATERLOO .. a		10 08	11 13								14 13					16 19	16 19

Heavy figures indicate through carriages
For general notes see page 49

For the train service between Exeter St. David's and North Devon and North Cornwall see Tables 59 and 73

For other trains between Exeter and St. James' Park Halt see Table 69

For the principal train service between London and Exeter see Table 1

A   Through train from Barnstaple Junction (dep. 7.05) to Exmouth (arr. 8.41)
C   Through train from Plymouth (via Okehampton) dep. 7.50
D   Through train from Padstow (dep. 8.48) and Okehampton (dep. 11.10)
E   Through train from Ilfracombe (dep. 7.00)
G   Through train and ⊗ from Plymouth (dep. 10.55) to Brighton (arr. 17.24)
H   Through train to Exmouth
J   Through train from Tavistock (dep. 7.10) to Exmouth (arr. 9.09)
K   Through train from Torrington (dep. 10.05) and Barnstaple Junction (dep. 10.38)

h   🚍 (Southern National) from Seaton Sea Front to Axminster

cancel trains and utilise buses, or seemingly leave passengers to make their own alternative arrangements as seems the norm nowadays, services were retained but diversions were necessary whilst the work was being undertaken. Hence on 2 April the 12:15 Exeter – Waterloo was diverted via Yeovil Pen Mill and Westbury where it had to reverse to reach Salisbury. Passengers for Sherborne and Gillingham being conveyed to their destinations by taxi from Yeovil Pen Mill. The first trains over the new single line section were on Sunday 2 April when the 15:54 from Waterloo headed by D814 *Dragon* crossed the 16:35 from Exeter at Gillingham headed by D808 *Centaur*.

General freight traffic between Exeter and Salisbury had also ceased by this time, although there remained some movements in the form of milk tank traffic from Seaton Junction and Chard Junction, stone traffic from Whimple to Portishead, whilst Yeovil Junction retained a permanent way depot. Coal traffic to Sidmouth from Sidmouth Junction also still operated twice weekly, whilst fertiliser traffic from Gillingham and the occasional MOD traffic from Dinton constituted the remaining freight operations, together with through ballast traffic from the quarry at Meldon to various SR destinations. However, this latter traffic was soon to be re-routed via the WR route to Taunton and

Table 2 — Weekdays

Exeter to Salisbury and London Waterloo

		A	✕	E				B		C	E	A	E
EXETER ST. DAVID'S .. d	13 07	13 46	14 20	15 43	...	16 45	...	17 20	17 37 ..	18 10	19 27 ...	19 30	20 16	22 02
EXETER CENTRAL .. a	13 10	13 49	14 23	15 46	...	16 48	...	17 23	17 40 ..	18 13	19 30 ...	19 34	20 19	22 05
69 EXMOUTH .. d	12 45	..	13 50	15 00	..	16 00	..	16 40	..	17 10	17 40 19 25			
EXETER CENTRAL .. d	13 18	...	14 25	15 48	...	16 51	...	17 25	..	17 42	18 15 20 00			
ST. JAMES' PARK HALT .. d	...	..	..	..	...	..	..	...	..	..				
PINHOE .. d	13 23	...	..	15 53	...	16 56	...	..	17 49	18 21 20 07				
BROAD CLYST .. d	13 28	..	..	15 56	...	17 01	...	..	17 53	18 24 20 11				
WHIMPLE .. d	13 35	..	..	16 01	...	17 08	...	..	18 00	18 31 20 18				
SIDMOUTH JUNCTION .. a	13 42	..	14 38	16 08	...	17 15	...	17 38	18 06	18 38 20 25				
68 SIDMOUTH .. a	14 07	..	15 13	..	16 50	..	17 40	..	18 28	..	18 28 19 00			
68 BUDLEIGH SALTERTON .. d	13 13	..	..	..	..	..	16 13	17 33	18 05					
68 SIDMOUTH .. d	13 20	..	14 13	15 40	..	..	16 58	17 44	17 44 19 53					
SIDMOUTH JUNCTION .. d	13 42	..	14 39	16 09	...	17 15	...	17 39	18 07	18 38 20 28				
HONITON .. d	13 50	..	14 50	16a17	...	17 24	...	..	18a15	18 45 20 37				
SEATON JUNCTION .. a	13 59	..	14 54	..	...	17 33	...	17 54	..	18 55 20 48				
67 SEATON .. a	14 13	..	15 10	..	18 07	..	18 07	..	19 22					
.. d	13 40	..	14 35	..	17 00	..	17 38	..	18 10 19 25					
SEATON JUNCTION .. d	13 59	..	14 54	..	17 34	..	17 54	..	18 56 20 50					
AXMINSTER .. a	14 05	..	15 01	..	17 39	..	18 01	..	19 01 20 55					
66 LYME REGIS .. a	14 28	..	..	..	..	..	18 26	..	19 23					
.. d	13 30	..	14 32	..	17 15	..	17 15	..	18 30 19b46					
AXMINSTER .. d	14 05	..	15 02	..	17 40	..	18 02	..	19 02 20 58					
CHARD JUNCTION .. d	14 14	..	..	..	17 49	..	..	19 11 21 08						
CREWKERNE .. d	14 25	..	..	..	18 01	..	18 20	..	19 24 21 20					
YEOVIL JUNCTION .. a	14 35	..	15 25	..	18 11	..	18 30	..	19 34 21 32					
61 YEOVIL TOWN .. a	14 42	..	15 35	..	18 18	..	18 38	..	19 42 21 45					
.. d	..	..	15 17	..	15 45 17 10 18 02	..	18 23	..	21 30					
YEOVIL JUNCTION .. d	..	..	15 26	..	15 55 17 17 18 12	..	18 30	..	21 42					
SHERBORNE .. d	..	..	15 36	..	16 03 17a24 18 21	..	18 40	..	21 50					
MILBORNE PORT HALT .. d	..	..	..	..	16 10 .. 18 28	..	..	..	21 59					
TEMPLECOMBE .. d	..	..	15 47	..	16 16 .. 18 34	..	18 51	..	22 07					
GILLINGHAM .. d	..	..	15 59	..	16 26 .. 18 44	..	19 01	..	22 17					
SEMLEY .. d	..	..	..	..	16 34 .. 18 52	..	..	..	22 27					
TISBURY .. d	..	..	..	..	16 41 .. 19 00	..	..	..	22 35					
DINTON .. d	..	..	..	..	16 48 .. 19 07	..	..	..						
WILTON SOUTH .. d	..	..	..	..	16 56 .. 19 15	..	..	..						
SALISBURY .. a	..	..	16 27	..	17 02 .. 19 21	..	19 30	..	22 52					
ANDOVER JUNCTION .. a	..	..	16 58	..	17 47	..	19 58	..	..					
BASINGSTOKE .. a	..	..	17 20	..	18 28	..	20 20	..	2 10					
WOKING .. a	..	..	17 46	..	19 46	..	20 46	..	2 49					
LONDON WATERLOO .. a	..	..	18 13	..	19 52	..	21 13	..	3 48					

Heavy figures indicate through carriages
For general notes see page 49

For the train service between Exeter St. David's and North Devon and North Cornwall see Tables 59 and 73

For other trains between Exeter and St. James' Park Halt see Table 69

For the principal train service between London and Exeter see Table 1

A Through train from Ilfracombe to Exmouth
B Through train from Ilfracombe to Budleigh Salterton.
C Through train from Plymouth (via Okehampton) dep. 17.15 to Eastleigh
E Through train from Ilfracombe

b (Southern National) from Lyme Regis (Langford's Shop)

Public timetable September 1964 to June 1965.

Westbury and thence to Salisbury. Elsewhere at this time station goods yards took on a dismal air as sidings were lifted or put out of use, whilst rusting tracks remained on the closed branches to Lyme Regis, Chard and Seaton.

The second phase of the singling commenced over the weekend of 6/7 May when the section from Sherborne to Chard Junction was dealt with, a distance of 21½ miles. Whilst the double track section between Templecombe and Sherborne catered for the passing of most services on the line, the up line was signalled for bi-directional working indicating that there would be occasions when Templecombe box was

switched out, leaving the section from Gillingham to Sherborne as a single line. West of Sherborne the former up line was in use as far as Yeovil Junction, whereas what had been the down line was regained and used as far as Crewkerne. From here, the up line was in use to Chard Junction. At Yeovil Junction the down platform was no longer used and consequently it was no longer possible for trains to pass here, surely an unnecessary restriction.

The third and final phase of singling took place between Chard Junction and Pinhoe over the weekend of 10/11 June and it is perhaps worth examining the detail of this phase as set out

Indicative of the problems which route singling can cause, is this view taken from a late running Exeter bound service just to the west of the former station at Templecombe. Held at the colour light signal is a 'Class 33' diesel with the through service to Brighton but is awaiting access to the single line eastwards to Gillingham. The site of the former up yard, now trackless, is visible on the right. These 'Crompton' diesels operated over the route, having taken over from the unreliable* Warships in 1971 until they were themselves superseded by the more powerful 'Class 50s' in 1980. (*Reliability issues were based mainly around the NBL rather than the Swindon built members of the class and involved bogie ride and turbo issues. Ironically reliability – this time complexities with the control circuitry – was the reason for unreliability of the 'Class 50' diesels in the 1980s.)

Goods Yard closures

Wilton	6-7-64	
Dinton	18-4-67	
Tisbury	18-4-66	
Semley		
Gillingham	5-4-65	
Templecombe	5-4-65	
Milborne Port		
Sherborne	18-4-66	
Yeovil Junction		
Sutton Bingham		
Crewkerne		
Chard Junction	3-10-66	Excluding milk
Axminster	1960	
Seaton Junction	8-5-67	Excluding milk
Honiton		
Sidmouth Junction	27-1-64	
Whimple	4-12-67	Excluding Whiteway's cider products
Broad Clyst	1965	
Pinhoe	10-6-67	Excluding cold store traffic

Pinhoe." Thus runs the preamble to WR notice S.2515 for 'Employees Only'. In four sections the details of the singling operation were spelled out. Section 1 concerned alterations to the permanent way and existing signalling. These were detailed at eleven different locations viz. Chard Junction, Broom Gates, Axe Gates, Axminster Gates, Seaton Junction, Honiton, Sidmouth Junction Ground Frame, Sidmouth Junction, Whimple, Crannaford Gates, and Pinhoe. To take just a couple of examples the changes were summarised thus –

CHARD JUNCTION

The existing main line trailing crossover will be recovered. The existing Down main line will be renamed "Down and Up". Loop and the existing Up Main line will be renamed the "Up and Down" Main.

A new motor worked facing connection will be provided in the single line, the hand crank will be kept in the signal box.

The Down Main Home signal with Junction indicator will now also read to "Up and Down" Main. The Junction indicator will not be displayed for this route.

in the BR 'Notice to Trainmen' opposite "Between the hours of 22:00 on Saturday 10 June and 23:00 on Sunday 11 June 1967 (or until completion) the Chief Signal & Telecoms Engineer will be engaged in introducing Stage 3 (Final) of the singling scheme and of the existing double line between Chard Junction and

The following new signals will be provided on the attached diagram on the next page:

G – Position Light Up Main to Loop

H – Down Main Starting

A "Train Arrival" plunger (Z) will be provided as shown on the attached diagram.

AXMINSTER GATES

The existing signals will apply to the Single line.

The signal box will be reduced in status to a Ground Frame.

A telephone connection to Chard Junction signal box will be provided.

The existing level crossing gates will be worked by a Crossing Keeper.

Section 2 of the Notice concerned the introduction of Tokenless Block Working (TBW) and merely stated that TBW in accordance with the "Regulations for Train Signalling on Single Lines by the TBW System" would be instituted between the following new Block Sections – Chard Junction to Honiton and Honiton to Pinhoe. Box to Box telephones will be provided.

Section 3 of the Notice stated that all AWS ramps between Wilton South and Exmouth Junction inclusive have been rendered inoperative.

Finally Section 4 of the Notice detailed the Occupation Arrangements, namely that engineer's occupation of the locking frames at Chard Junction, Honiton, Sidmouth Junction Ground Frame and Pinhoe would be required for alterations and testing purposes. During such occupation all distant signals will be disconnected from the signal boxes and maintained at Caution. All arrangements for safe working of the line including the appointment of any hand signalmen lie with the District Inspector based at Exeter Central.

PRIVATE and not for Publication   NOTICE No. S.2515

BRITISH RAILWAYS

(WESTERN REGION)

(For the use of employees only)

Notice to Trainmen, etc.

SALISBURY—EXETER, SINGLING OF LINE

(STAGE 3—CHARD JUNCTION TO PINHOE)

SATURDAY AND SUNDAY
10th AND 11th JUNE 1967

Between the hours of 22.00 on Saturday, 10th June, and 23.00 on Sunday, 11th June 1967 (or until completion), the Chief Signal and Telecommunications Engineer will be engaged in introducing Stage 3 (Final) of the above scheme consisting of the singling of the existing double line between Chard Junction and Pinhoe, in accordance with the attached diagram.

Chard Junction signal box with the new signal bracket and the bi-directional running lines of the Chard loop.

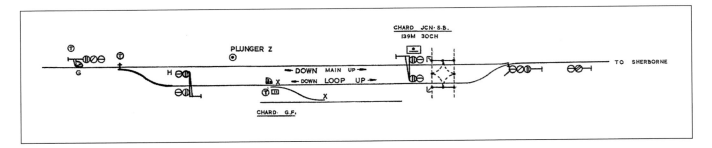

In summary then, this third phase saw the passing loop at Chard Junction enabled to permit bi-directional running over both tracks. Approaching Axminster, the single track using the former up line was slewed to the down line as the main station buildings at Axminster station were on that side. From here to Pinhoe the former down line was used. Honiton had a passing loop also with bi-directional running and at Whimple, although the former down line was in use, the former up line, where the main building was located, was retained through the station to act as a shunting neck. It was reported in the enthusiast's press of the time that the trains used during these engineering works were of varied formation depending upon the specific requirements. A brake van was located at each end of the train and even an old Hawksworth tender was noted in the rake.

THINK AGAIN

Experience gained in operating over the sections of single line resulted in the reinstatement of 4½ miles of double track between Sherborne and Yeovil Junction within months of the singling on 1 October 1967 and in an effort to reduce the often significant delays that had been occurring. The effects of one derailment, resulting from a down newspaper train which had just left Sherborne and had entered the single line at excessive speed, resulted in the route being blocked for four days. The possible effects of this derailment were only ameliorated by recourse to bringing back into use the second track, which was fortuitously still in position at this point, and was then used by the engineers clearing the blockage.

Adverse reports in the railway press were also frequent, indicating that timekeeping was poor on the route even before the final phase of singling. On 26 May, for example, down trains were running extremely late, the 15:00 from Waterloo arriving at Exeter Central some 64 minutes late, whilst the 17:00 from Waterloo was 30 minutes down on schedule by the time it reached Chard Junction. On 11 June, the date of completion of the singling scheme, the 12:25 from Exeter arrived at Honiton 28 minutes late, in turn causing delay to the 08:45 from Waterloo which had to wait 10 minutes in the loop at Honiton. To compound the delays even further, this same down train came to grief shortly after by suffering a complete locomotive failure on the single line and was only rescued after a delay of two hours. A circular letter was issued by BR to long-suffering passengers during the first week, thanking them for their tolerance during recent months and promising better things for the future. In addition to motive power failures the institution of the tokenless block signalling system apparatus also saw its share of equipment failures.

The singling scheme might have stood a better chance of success had the by then unreliable 'Warship' diesels not been the chosen primary motive power. By August, timekeeping remained poor with 'Warship' failures often necessitating replacement locomotives in the form of the lower powered D65xx 'Cromptons' and D7xxx 'Hymeks' which understandably struggled to keep to the schedules. By mid-August, track recovery was being carried out along various stretches of former double track, in some cases completely and in other cases merely the rails having been removed. In this month,

Schematic diagram of running lines and loops.

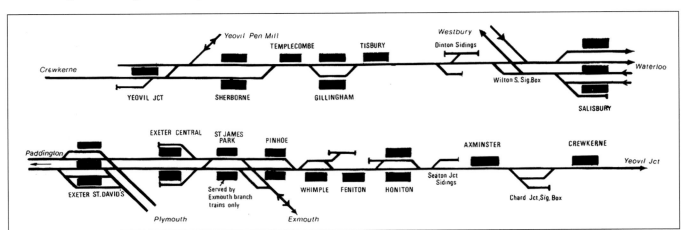

recovery was proceeding along the Axminster to Seaton Junction section using D4021 hauling wagons upon which the recovered rails were loaded. Sleepers and rails were also being stockpiled at Yeovil Junction. Waterloo also dictated that up trains were to be given priority over down trains, this no matter how late the latter were, all in an effort to keep interference with SR trains east of Basingstoke at a minimum.

WAS THERE AN ALTERNATIVE TO THE SINGLING?

The major benefits of the singling were claimed to be cost savings resulting from the maintenance of fewer miles of track and consequent lower track renewal costs. This argument does not hold as much water as one might expect, for until the end of 1962, the SR had maintained the route to the highest main line standards and many miles of track had been fairly recently re-laid, some with continuously welded rail (cwr). With the reduced level of traffic then proposed, necessary renewals would not have been significant for several years. A double track line could also have been retained with reduced signalling commensurate with a two-hourly semi-fast service. Probably only three signal boxes would have been required to control the whole 90 miles between Exeter and Salisbury i.e. at Salisbury, Yeovil Junction and Exmouth Junction. As it was, boxes at Pinhoe, Honiton, Chard Junction, Templecombe, Gillingham and Wilton had to remain open, some of them virtually continuously, to control points and signals which resulted in an inflated signalling wages bill. But behind the scenes there was actually a government incentive for the BR Regions to reclaim as much 'surplus' track as possible as grants increased according to how much redundant track they were

able to recover. *(The WR divisional offices at Reading, the now demolished 'Western Tower' alongside the station, had a 'Redundant Assets' section within the CCE department and no doubt other divisions had likewise. Remember too, this was a time when managers might receive a bonus commensurate on how much they could save by removing facilities.)*

Whilst the benefit of reclaiming the second track for scrap or for re-use elsewhere would have been lost had the double line remained in place, on the plus side would have been the cost saving through not undertaking the singling operation with associated civil engineering and signalling costs, a reduction in point wear at each passing loop, and a reduction in wear and tear on two lines, for with only one track remaining serving both up and down trains, wear was in effect doubled. Of the four signal boxes that were required to be open continuously, there were no other duties for the signalmen to perform at Templecombe and Wilton South, both stations having closed to passengers. In retaining double track, perhaps most importantly there would have been the flexibility to adapt to future changed circumstances in that increases in service frequency could much more easily have been accommodated on two tracks rather than one.

IMPROVEMENTS

Not all has been retrenchment during our period of review however, as the following improvements have taken place. Sidmouth Junction station, closed five years before, re-opened as Feniton, which had indeed been its name when originally opened. This re-opening took place on 3 May 1971 and was intended to serve the rapid expansion of housing developments in the vicinity. It remains open today.

Typical of a singled section of the route is this view of the closed station at Semley which formerly served the hilltop town of Shaftesbury. Intending rail passengers now had to make their way by bus or car the eight miles to Gillingham, which acted as the railhead for the surrounding area.

Yeovil Junction seen in the late 1960s when the station footbridge was still complete although, as referred to in the text, the former down platform had been taken out of use and only the up platform was used for all services. The lack of a passing facility at the up platform is readily apparent and it was not to be until 1975 that trains could once again pass here. The former up through road has been partly recovered in this view.

Sensibly, services were again able to pass at Yeovil Junction from 26 March 1975 adding to operational flexibility. Then, on 18 May 1983, Pinhoe station re-opened followed closely by Templecombe on 3 October the same year, the latter facility aided to a great extent by the Salisbury Area Manager, Gerry Daniels. At a cost of £435,000 a loop near Tisbury was laid in on 24 March 1986. Unfortunately this had to be done on the formation some distance from the station as the former down platform was no longer available to BR who had sold off the land some years before.

Finally a new diesel depot, to service the Class 159 units, was opened on 12 June 1993 at Salisbury. Further improvements, such as the opening of the Axminster loop and the increase in service frequency, have followed in the period after 1993.

LBSCR Engineer's Photographs of 1907

David Wigley

We were recently loaned a small parcel of what are officially taken views of LBSCR engineering subjects recorded in the South London area by acknowledged expert David Wigley. David has kindly taken the time to research and record both the locations and some interesting facts surrounding several. In his own words:

I was puzzled by this location for a long time until able to confirm my original thoughts that it is Norwood Fork junction on the down local lines; left to West Croydon and East Croydon, and right to Selhurst. The distracting factor was the signal but this has no relation to the tracks in view. It is actually at natural ground level controlling traffic on the up local line which passes under the flyover. The purpose of the photograph is to record the switch which has been 'run through' from the Selhurst direction. There is damage to both switch rails and gauge has been temporarily restored with tie bars. The switch has a facing point controlled through a fouling bar on the left hand rail plus detectors for two of the signals behind the photographer. Also in the distance are two electric fouling bars to advise the signalman when a train has cleared the junction. Finally there is a typical LBSCR gradient post on the left.

From the same position but this time with the points reversed. Neither of the routes visible exist today in the form seen.

A progress record of the switch cabin at Denmark Hill (as shown complete on p6 of *The LBSCR Elevated Electrification* – Noodle Books.)

Electrification progress looking East between Denmark Hill and Peckham Rye Junction. Visible are the Up LBSCR and Down SECR distant signals. The photograph was taken from the LBSCR lines with those of the SECR as the pair on the left.

Electrification progress looking East approximately mid-way between Denmark Hill and Peckham Rye. Again the pair of SECR lines is in the immediate foreground.

LBSCR electrification progress and this time the photographer has moved to look East from Clapham from the East end of the viaduct over Bedford Road. A pair of LBSCR lines are to the right with the three to the left used by the SECR.

An earlier view of the electrification works near to Dol Street (Ferndale Road) footbridge taken adjacent to the signal bracket for the SECR up lines as shown on p17 of 'The LBSCR Elevated Electrification'. Stay wires for the brackets are also visible.

Above: **Taken further West and approaching the viaduct over Bedford Road and Clapham High Street – the East end of Clapham station. (This is the opposite view to that of p6 in 'The LBSCR Elevated Electrification'.)**

Right: **Annotated as 'The Windsor Castle public house Clapham Junction'. The Windsor Castle faces on to St John's Hill, Battersea, and presumably had to be part demolished to provide a site for the new LBSCR entrance. (See 'London Railway Record No 85, October 2015, p305.) The pub survives and sports a c1930 mock Tudor frontage.**

Annotated 'Earlswood Slip', noticeable is the effect of the ground heave on the siding track in the first two views. The third view shows a 'tell-tale' across a crack in the concrete retaining wall to detect further movement. Also to the right is a drop hammer piling frame lying on its working face and about to be pulled upright on to the two timber baulks to undertake some remedial work. The final view is of houses on the North side of St John's Road, Earlswood, standing on rising ground above the railway. This suggests a claim for the visible repairs in the picture. It cannot have been too serious as the houses exist today.

Opposite: **These two views depict another slip in South London, this time on an embankment. The railway boundary fence has been displaced and timber piles which had been driven in an attempt to control the situation have also moved. The houses seen are in Elderton Road, SE16.**

The final images are around the Kensington and Chelsea Cottage Home School at Banstead and appear to be recording a dispute over the maintenance of the boundary hedge by the South side of the line. In the first view we see the Epsom Downs down distant signal and a glimpse of the end parapet of the Drift Bridge spanning Reigate Road (now the A240) plus further away still, the buffer stop of a siding at Epsom Down. In the second view we are looking towards Banstead with the buildings of the school behind the trees. Some wagons are visible in a private siding serving an estate North of the railway with a trailing connection from the up line. Next we have a general view of the down line recently relayed with 96lb per yard LBSCR material. The up line is of the earlier 75lb rail. Also of comment is that there is no ballast supporting the sleeper ends, totally contrary to current practice. Finally there is a view of the railway near to what was a playground, the LBSCR being concerned over children accessing the railway – had there perhaps been an accident? (Kensington and Chelsea Cottage Home School was closed in 1974 with the land now a residential area known as High Beeches.)

The Fall and Rise of the SECR Steamship *Onward*

David Austin

Vue Générale (Turbine "Onward"), Boulogne-sur-Mer

Commercial French postcard of the *Onward* at Boulogne at the start of her service in 1905.

In 1918 the SECR railway steamer and military troopship *Onward* was scuttled in Folkestone harbour. The salvage operation has many similarities to the more recent recovery of the *Costa Concordia* except that several railway engines were used to pull the *Onward* upright before re-floating it. This article looks at the background of SECR railway steamships, their use in the movement of troops during wartime, and an outline of how the raising of the *Onward* might even be modelled. As a mariner, I was particularly interested in understanding the user interface between land-based steam motive power and the waterlogged marine steam ship.

Folkestone and preparing for the Great War

The small fishing port of Folkestone has the geographic privilege of being one of the ports closest to the French coast, and, being a natural harbour, became an obvious location for the earliest communication systems with the European continent. It is recorded that King Henry inspected the harbour in 1543 and in 1710, prior to the development of electric communications, it was the home of the Pigeon Post. Subsequently, the headquarters of the Stock Exchange were built in the harbour to transmit and receive stock prices between London and the continental capitals over the copper wires of the telegraph and telephone. The scent of money brought the wealthy gentlemen to the small town, and by building stately homes on the West Cliffs, created a mini leisure resort. Unfortunately a regular procession of violent storms, recorded first in 1705, served to wipe out the fishing fleet on many occasions. It was thought of vital importance to preserve the only industry in the harbour and these disasters led to the construction of the first protection breakwater in 1806.

As the modest town assumed the air of 'upmarketness', the harbour was developed between 1807 and 1818 to cater for the berthing of ever larger cross channel steamers and for protection from the famed Channel weather. In the Great War, the town became the home of the first intelligence HQ, a haven for the thousands of refugees from France and Belgium, and the last home port for thousands of troops who are remembered with the marching order 'Short Step'.

The role of the South Eastern Railway

The SER was enacted in 1836 for the purpose of establishing a line of communication from London to Paris through the channel ports. A route was selected through the middle of Kent, passing through Ashford and terminating in Folkestone. The railway was completed in 1843, and having pushed the track work right through into the harbour, trains had to negotiate a fearsome incline and 150 foot gap to reach the ferry berths on the pier. Within the next five years, the railway company purchased the harbour and several steamships, had opened the first purpose built hotel (the 'South Eastern Pavilion' by William Cubitt) for cross channel passengers, had built the largest swing bridge in the country, and in 1848 had started the inaugural cross channel railway service from London to Paris, via Folkestone and Boulogne.

Carrying the Troops

Nineteenth-century Britain controlled an Empire which ranged across the entire globe and as a result, had become very experienced in the need to maintain her armed forces in far off lands. As early as 1833 during the Portuguese Civil War, the founders of what became the P&O shipping line began to use steam paddle ships for the transport of troops. Six ships were chartered and used to embark Portuguese troops at Oporto to invade southern Portugal. Until the coming of steam, the time taken by troopships on passage to Africa and particularly to India, combined with their uncertain date of arrival, had always involved unavoidable difficulties. By the early 1850s however, there was no shortage of passenger ships available to carry troops overseas, but most of the early British steamship companies had been able to begin operations only with the aid of a Government subsidy. This financial assistance was given solely on the understanding that the companies were to allow their ships to be used as troopships by the government in wartime. The Crimean War of 1854 was a major exercise in large scale movements of troops but the Indian Mutiny in 1857 put even more strain on the trooping transport service. The bunker capacity of many commercial ships was also limiting the range of these force projections to distant lands. The famous sinking of *HMS Birkenhead* off the South African coast in 1852 gave rise to the age-old precedence of 'women and children first' as 500 soldiers on the sinking ship refused to overwhelm the small number of lifeboats which were saving the lives of thirty-one women and children.* The military troopship came of age when five specially-designed vessels were built in 1866 to carry troops between Great Britain and India.

The greatest test for the transport services came in 1914 when the scale of war grew to even greater levels. Before the outbreak, the Government had considered the possibility of having to land an Expeditionary Force in Belgium and a committee consisting of the heads of Cunard, Royal Mail, White Star, Blue Funnel and P&O was set up to formulate practical plans. On the outbreak of war, a Royal Proclamation authorised the Admiralty to requisition 250

* In similar vein, more men lost their lives on the Titanic by ensuring their wives and children entered the lifeboats first. One recent radio account of the latter's 1912 sinking recalled how, after seeing their loved ones lowered to safety, their menfolk might be observed chatting and smoking cigars whilst chaos ensued all around.

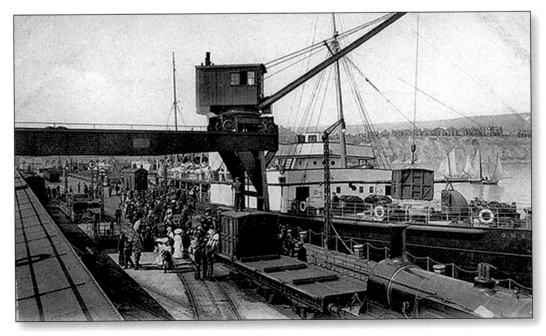

Commercial postcard of the *Onward* leaving Folkestone soon after 1905.

Aerial view of the capsized *Onward* with a salvage ship alongside before the funnels and deck houses were removed to allow lifting. *Courtesy of the IWM*

merchant ships as transports. Although there was a certain amount of confusion, an Expeditionary Force of 210,000 officers and men, 6,200 horses and 100,000 tons of ammunition had been landed within a period of sixteen days, three days earlier than planned. But this was small fry compared with the total for four years of WWI, when the Transport Department provided for the passages of 23,700,000 individual troops in addition to the millions of tons of stores, munitions and equipment. After the war, the huge task of repatriating the British, Dominion and Allied troops was carried out, principally by British ships.

By 1914, the harbour at Folkestone and its facilities had been expanded to cope with increased volumes of traffic from larger and faster cross channel ferries. At the dawn of the Great War, the railway in the harbour had settled down to a busy existence of carrying the mails, various goods and many passengers on their way to and from 'The Other Side'. Over the course of the conflict, the railway had to cope with an extraordinary amount of additional war-time traffic. John Carlile (see end reference 'Folkestone During The War 1914-1919') has recorded that 7,000 military trains conveyed nearly 11 million soldiers and workers, and 550,000 tons of freight through the harbour ; and this in addition to the fact that throughout the war, the railway kept its running of regular services with 8,500 trains and a fleet of railway ships.

Troopships – *Onward* from Peace to War

It is not surprising that many of the small and efficient railway steamers, manned by well-trained seamen, were requisitioned early in the war. During the conflict they carried across the Channel the troops, horses, artillery, munitions and stores of every kind. In addition, many crosschannel steamers which were not themselves required to maintain essential services were commandeered either as HM troopships (HMT) or as hospital ships in the early months of the war. To the surprise of many professional sailors also, the London pleasure steamers proved to be fine sea boats and did magnificent work during the war as crosschannel troopers. The first to be requisitioned was the *Golden Eagle* and during her three years on active service she carried over 500,000 troops of various nations without loss.

Onward with dazzle camouflage in evidence tied to the pier to prevent movement by the tide flowing in and out of the harbour. *Courtesy of the IWM*

The specific subject of this piece, the *Onward,* was built at William Denny and Brothers shipyard, Dumbarton, in 1905 for the SECR. She was a steel, triple-screw turbine-driven vessel with a length of 311 feet and 2 inches and a beam of 40 feet. Her accommodation was for a crew of 70 and she was certificated to carry 1,479 passengers. Her Parsons turbine engines developed 7,500hp to provide a service speed of 22 knots. In 1905, she carried King Edward VII from Dover to Calais on one of his frequent European tours and she had the distinction of carrying the very first motor car across the English Channel.

On 24 August 1918 the *Onward* was berthed on the new southern pier in Folkestone preparing to load troops. During the night a thermite bomb was planted in a lifeboat by a saboteur. When it exploded the resulting fire spread throughout the ship and in an effort to save her, she was scuttled at the railway berth to settle on her port side in the shallow waters of the harbour. The salvage operation was attempted within weeks and by using railway engines on the pier to steady the recovery effort was successful in righting her. The *Onward* was repaired and re-entered service as the *Mona's Isle*.

Dunkirk 1940

By the time the steamships of the Southern Railway were called into active service again in 1939, the *Mona's Isle* (nee *Onward*) was 34 years old and was considered to be an old ship. Like many other cross channel passenger ships, she was fitted out as an Armoured Boarding Vessel and for the first few months of the war her life was largely uneventful but by the end of May 1940 the plight of the British Expeditionary Force (BEF) in France was becoming a national disaster. The *Mona's Isle* joined seven of her cross channel sisters to make passage to Dunkirk and was the first ship to leave Dover to pick up troops. She returned on the next day with 1,420 troops and made a second round trip to finally rescue a total of 2,634 troops. Following service in the Newcastle area she was a troop and store ship after D-Day until June 1945, when she was then chartered by the Ministry of War Transport before she was finally released from her war service in March 1946. The *Mona's Isle* (nee *Onward*) was scrapped at Milford Haven in October of 1948.

Raising the Onward

Following her deliberate scuttling, she lay on her port side in shallow water close to the wall of the southern pier. Fortunately at least half of the ship was visible and accessible to the salvage team. There appears to have been no damage to the integrity of the hull plates and the ship was intact apart from internal fire damage. Decades later, the *Costa Concordia* was an entirely different proposition, having suffered a large split in the hull below the waterline and was also resting on the side of a precipitous underwater cliff. However the salvage operations for the two ships had similarities. The basic approach to salvage at sea is to make the hull watertight and floatable, to keep the ship upright and to take the ship to a place of safety for repair.

The pictures of the capsized *Onward* provide several clues to the salvage operation. The cables are laid out to suggest that the sequence of events could have been to: bring a tug and barge alongside, remove funnels and deckhouses to allow barge to connect air compressor equipment for pumping out the flood water. Divers on board to close the seacocks and to create as many watertight compartments within the hull as possible. Connect cables from the port (underwater) side to five railway engines on the pier via sheer legs. At low water, pump out the watertight compartments and allow the rising tide to lift the hull to an upright position. The pulling power of the railway engines being used to keep tension on the lifting cables and to support the hull in the right position. Continue to pump out the other internal spaces and re-float the ship.

References and Sources

John Charles Carlile:
'*Folkestone During The War 1914-1919*' Pub 2015: these figures are quoted: – 9,253,652 British officers and men; 537,523 other Allied troops; 846,919 Red Cross and other workers; 102,641 tons of military and Red Cross freight; 383,098 tons of mail and parcels; 63,985 tons of Expeditionary Force Canteens; 402,968 tons of coal were handled to power the vessels using the port.

RG Robertson:
Series of articles tracing the history of British troopships in war and peace.

History Online, Ruth Parkinson:
http://www.ruthparkinson.co.uk/fhslarge8.html

John Hendy:
'*Folkestone – Boulogne 1843 – 1991*'.

John de S Winser:
BEF Ships. 1999, World Ship Society.

The salvage operation is ready to start. The funnels and deck houses have been removed from the *Onward*. The cable running to the sheer legs on the pier is connected to the railway engines.

EMU Recognition Part 1

Richard Whitbread

Finishing touches being made to the station of the Waterloo & City Railway at Waterloo in 1898. The space constraints imposed are obvious whilst the presence of the supporting pillar also dictated the necessity for segregated arrival and departure platforms although a combined arch spanned the connections to the reversing siding and depot roads. The centre conductor rail will be noted.

In recent issues of *Southern Way* there have been comments and queries on various aspects and histories of the Southern (and earlier) multiple units – and the SEG has offered to provide a series of articles covering the range of electric and diesel-electric multiple units which have appeared on Southern metals. Whilst we shall largely follow a chronological history we may deviate if any particular units come up for discussion. It is not intended to give a complete unit history in detail but to look at individual classes of units and how the breed developed over the last (almost) 120 years.

You may first ask 'Why 120 years'? Well, the first electrically powered passenger carrying vehicles were built for the (sort of) independent Waterloo and City Railway at Eastleigh Works from a kit of parts shipped from Jackson and Sharp Company of Wilmington in the USA, entering service on 8 August 1898 when the W & C line opened.

	Length	Width floor level	Width at roof level	Height from rail level	Wheelbase	Bogie centres
Motor Cars	47ft 1in	8ft 6in	7ft 10in	9ft 8in	6ft	25ft 6in
Trailer Cars	46ft 3.5 in	8ft 6in	7ft 10in	9ft 8in	5ft 6in	25ft 6in

Height was a problem – the basic body frame had 5inches of clearance to the tunnel ceiling but with the power cables running along the roof (see below), clearance was reduced to just 1.75 inches.

There were 12 motor cars (1-12) and 10 trailer cars (21-30), all of which were open saloons – the absence of compartments a little unusual at the time. Operating formation was motor-trailer-trailer-motor. Buffing was by a central buffer-coupling. There were hand operated collapsible iron gate entrances at the end of each trailer and the trailer end of the motor cars. The trailers seated 56 persons, and the motor coaches seated 46, with a raised section over the motor bogie. The first set reached Waterloo on 4 March 1898 and a successful test run was completed on 4 June 1898.

The traction motors by Siemens (who were responsible for the electrical aspects of the line) were series-wound 60hp (45kW) gearless motors on the axles which were supplied by Cammell & Co and the Kitson's system wheels were supplied by Leeds Wheel and Axle Co1. The trains were fitted with roller bearings.

There was one powered bogie on each motor car with two axle hung traction motors under the driver's cab. (Another reference refers to these being 42bhp rated at 70 amps and it being a 6" diameter axle.) The wheels were cast steel covered on the tread with a layer of teak wood and the running tyre was forced onto this wooden resilient layer and held in place with bolts and retaining rings. The bogies were mounted onto the coaches with a central pivot.

The motor cars were constructed to allow a form of multiple unit operation with the controller in the front car controller being able to control all motors. The two motors at each end were connected in series at starting but changed to parallel as the train accelerated. To achieve this control, eight cables were run along the length of the train at roof level. A further power cable linked the cast iron collector shoes together and intended to overcome problems with the large gaps in the centrally mounted conductor rail. The controller was also large as the full power supply was routed through it. There were eight working positions on the controller which operated as follows:

On the surface, stored and pending disposal; note the conductor shoes have been removed. The location is believed to be Horley where the redundant stock remained for some time. The original livery of the trains had been dark brown, later altered to SR green with full lining out and in their final days, plain green. Unusually, red was used for the colour of both the headlight and tail-lamp. At peak times, all five 5-car sets operated at 3-minute headway, the labour intensive nature of the operating meaning that a conductor was provided in each car to issue bell-punch type tickets. (Two conductors travelled on the single cars during off-peak times but still at a 5-10 minute interval working.) The journey time was 5½-6½ minutes although it could take a further 10-12 minutes for passengers to exit the station at the end of the journey via the subway then provided. Improvements in these areas did not finally occur until 1960. The power cars were numbered 1-12 and the trailers 21-36. Sets were identified by a letter, and comprised (in early 1940) the following, Set A: 10, 21, 22, 23, 9, Set B: 8, 24, 25, 26, 5, Set C: 6, 27, 28, 29, 12, Set D: 4, 31 ,32, 33, 2, Set E: 3, 34, 35, 36, 11. At the time the spare vehicles were thus Nos. 1, 7, 30. The single unit cars were numbered 13-17.

Position	Resistances	Motors
1	All	4 in series
2	Half	4 in series
3	None	4 in series
4	Half	2 in series in parallel with 2 in series
5	Quarter	2 in series in parallel with 2 in series
6	None	2 in series in parallel with 2 in series
7	Quarter	4 in parallel
8	None	4 in parallel

Initially there was a total crew of six: driver, driver's assistant, guard and three gatemen; after a while the assistant was felt to be no longer required. (The first 'single-manning' of a train perhaps?)

The trains used Westinghouse brakes with the air reservoirs having 30cu ft capacity and were charged from static compressors at Waterloo. They initially held 100psi, and could run down to 70psi before needing to be recharged. Typically this was enough air for 20 journeys between being recharged. Waterloo was equipped with compressed air standpipes driven by three pumps and there were a further two pumps on standby. Lighting was run off the power circuit, with four lamps in series from the 500V nominal.

A motor car in 'undressed state'. Built in the US, the term used was 'subway' car. Fitting out, along with other rather important details – such as the roof – have yet to be added. ACF Industries Inc.

In the manufacturer's yards at Wilmington, Delaware, trailer No 21 is seen, on what are clearly accommodation bogies, allowing the vehicle to be moved outside for the benefit of the photographer. This was no doubt a view taken in the course of construction as again the roof has still to be added. The extra large sheet of timber was a variation in removing the background to the photograph, an alternative to the 'painting-out' process sometimes adopted, but was surely extremely difficult to move as it is clearly only a temporary feature at that location.

Believed to be the interior of a trailer coach around the time of withdrawal. Do we take it the seats are of shaped timber or might that even be leather upholstery?

Operationally they were capable of more but the Board of Trade insisted on a limit of 15 mph due to the five chain radius curve at Stamford Street which was at the point where the trains should have been hitting a higher speed to minimise power consumption – if 29.5 mph had been permitted, journey time would have been about five minutes and power consumed reduced by a third compared to running at 15 mph maximum.

Traffic growth post the Great War led to a decision to enhance the trains to five cars with the construction of six new trailer cars (31-36), this time built at Eastleigh but to the same 1898 design. At the same time, signal changes were made to allow for a service every three minutes, which implies 20 trains per hour, although there is also mention of 24 trains per hour. (There is some conflict in the sources used; one says that there were originally 11 motors and 11 trailers; but there were definitely 12 motors. A further source says only four additional trailers were constructed (33-36) – but in total there were 16 and it is not therefore clear when 31 & 32 were built if not with the latter four.)

The original level of service provision was a train every five minutes – 12 per hour provided by four sets each of four cars – but was quickly identified to be in excess of passenger requirements between the peaks and after considering a number of possibilities, the railway placed an order for five single Dick, Kerr cars for use off peak, these having a driving compartment at each end. These were very similar in size to the individual coach sizes quoted above and were built with half-width cabs and two external sliding doors on each side and 50 seats. 75hp nose suspended motors were used and with a weight of just 26.5 tons the cars were able to accelerate faster, leading to a need for only three cars in service for the timetable. Running costs were significantly lower as not only were there no trailers but also the staff numbers needed were lower. The single cars were numbered 13-17.

This first W & C line stock was all removed from service in 1940 when replacement stock was constructed which we shall cover later.

Opposite top: **Interior of a trailer car under construction.**

Opposite bottom: **Complete interior of a motor coach but viewed around the time of withdrawal. Of note are the enclosed driver's compartment and different levels between the central compartment and seats over the bogies. Note the door far right affording access to the next car and notwithstanding the comments about overcrowding there are no straps or handrails for use of standing passengers.**

Car No 3 on an unknown date and likewise location. In 1940 this vehicle formed part of set 'E'.

The Southern Electric Group has been in existence for over 45 years and is responsible for the preservation of the only complete pre-war main line electric multiple unit, '4 Cor' 3142. Our magazine *Live Rail* has covered most units which have operated and this will provide some of the input into this series. You can find out more about the SEG at www.southernelectric.org.uk

Source references:

'Waterloo and City Railway' by Nigel Pennick.
    Published by Electric Traction Publications.

'The Waterloo & City Railway' by John C. Gilham.
    Published by The Oakwood Press.

The Lost Archives of Stephen Townroe
Part 11

I t is partly holiday time with this instalment as SCT took a trip by the GWR route towards the West Country (*which we thought best not to include*) before venturing on and off the beaten track...

SCT's trip to the West Country involved travel on the GWR line across the Saltash bridge and then venturing as far west as Bodmin Road. After this, it appears he went north to Bodmin General and then on, using the connection to the Southern at Wadebridge, where this view shows 'O2' No 203 arriving with a train from Padstow. The train is just about to pass over Molesworth Street level crossing with the signalman at the West signal box preparing to accept the tablet for the section from Padstow. Just visible behind the train and to the right are the sidings at Wadebridge Quay.

At some point during his trip, SCT was also by the lineside at Starcross to record a Southern 'Light Pacific' on a GWR train bound for Exeter. As is likely well known, SR engines had certain turns over the GW line between Plymouth and Exeter and GWR engines would similarly work some SR trains over the Southern line via Okehampton. This was to maintain route knowledge for crews in the event of necessary diversions.

Fireman's view from the cab of a 'West Country' 'somewhere' on the Barnstaple line. The engine is showing clear evidence of a previous casing fire. Meanwhile a 'T9' approaches with what may well be a Torrington line train.

Three views of the 'Devon Belle'. Firstly we see the Up train paused at Exeter St Davids while an 'E1/R' 0-6-2T arrives to assist the service up the bank through to Exeter Central. Note the menu in the holder at the rear of the front seat... Next we have a view inside the car whilst on the move. One might even say it gives a whole new meaning to the phrase, '...wanting to sit with one's back to the engine' – especially if there was a banker on at the time as well! Although classified a 'Pullman' observation car, the seats are definitely not the upholstered luxury that might be expected in a Pullman. This was deliberate and intended to discourage passengers from sitting in the observation coach for the whole of the journey. Whilst reservations were possible, indeed desirable within the main train, it was not possible to reserve a seat in the observation car. Finally the first of a small group of views taken of passing trains near Byfleet including the 'Devon Belle'. We may wonder perhaps if there might even have been a slight wistfulness at seeing the luxury train pass especially as at the time (May 1947 – April 1948) the Pullman service was one of the few places where a meal might be obtained without the restrictions of rationing.

We now have two further views at the same (Byfleet) location but without detail identification. The first of these is clearly a 'Urie' 'King Arthur' and appears to be No 450 *Sir Kay*. The headcode is for a West of England service consisting of both Maunsell and LSWR stock. In the second view we have what is a train seemingly of all LSWR stock pulled by 'U' No 1623. The headcode here is slightly more difficult to confirm but it may well be a Southampton Docks boat train – armed forces perhaps? [it is definitely No. 1623]

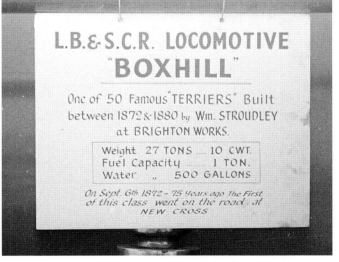

L.B.& S.C.R. LOCOMOTIVE
"BOXHILL"

One of 50 Famous "TERRIERS" Built between 1872 & 1880 by Wm. STROUDLEY at BRIGHTON WORKS.

Weight	27 TONS 10 CWT.
Fuel Capacity	1 TON.
Water ,,	500 GALLONS

On Sept. 6th 1872 - 75 Years ago The First of this class went on the road at NEW CROSS

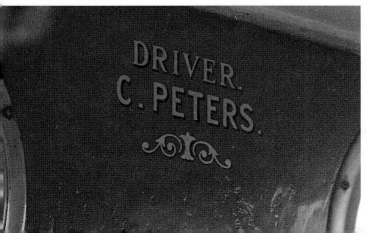

In 1947 the Southern Railway decided to preserve and repaint a former LBSCR 'Terrier', No 82, in the colours it had once displayed. The name originally carried, *Boxhill*, was likewise restored. The refurbished engine emerged from Brighton Works on 2 September and was first of all taken to the nearby running shed. The following day it was steamed and ran under its own power to Horsham en-route to Dorking North where it was on display along with electric loco CC2 in the goods yard for three days, Dorking North station being the nearest location to the actual place the 'Terrier' was named after: Box Hill. It is seen here in detail complete with explanatory text. On 11 September, No 82 was noted stored under sheeting at Nine Elms. The November issue of the 'R.O.' subsequently reported that the engine had been destined (and perhaps even restored) to travel to Switzerland to take part in the Swiss Railway Centenary but that the necessary arrangements could not finally be made.

Obviously a visit to Brighton where what is stated to be No 21C166 (later named *Spitfire*) was under construction. (This engine was released to traffic on 5 September 1947.)

On 15 June 1947 (SCT's negatives are slightly out of date order at this point, reference the earlier views of No 82), there was a 'derailment' at Chertsey. 'S15' No 502 passed signals at danger and collided with what was fortunately only an empty electric set. SCT provides no further detail whilst the excellent 'Railways Archive' site and other sources checked provide no detail other than to note that one person was injured. (On the same date but some thousands of miles away in Argentina a passenger train collided with a cow but with far more tragic consequences to a number of passengers.) Although damage and debris are visibly considerable, the locomotive must have come off lightly as there is no record of a works visit subsequent to this time. Again the public are keen to observe wherever possible.

As a professional engineer SCT was involved in observations away from his native Southern Railway, one of which is seen here where he noted the preparations for a dynamometer trial of an LNER 'B1' at Liverpool Street. We have a view of the dynamometer car, which vehicle was later used for testing on the Interchange trials of 1948 although this could well have been an earlier 'unofficial' or unrelated test as records do not appear to show a formal 'B1' test with this car starting from this location. Notice the weighed coal and the temporary fitment of an external tender water gauge – the latter in the form of the vertical pipe partly obscuring the 'E' of the initials on the tender. Note too the various connections from the top of the tender running to the cab roof. Decent coal was also obviously a priority with further supplies bagged ready for use. Together with the weighing of ashes, clinker and the coal remaining in the firebox at the end of a run, a record of coal used could thus be calculated: coal per mile, etc.

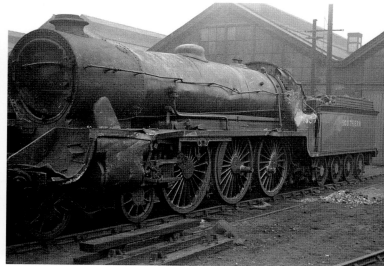

At 6.05 pm on 26 November 1947 a rear-end collision occurred between two Up passenger trains just west of Farnborough station. The trains concerned were the 3.05 pm from Bournemouth West to Waterloo carrying approximately 200 passengers and the 12.15 Ilfracombe to Waterloo with around 400 passengers. Respectively in charge were 'Lord Nelson' No 860 and 'King Arthur' No 453. The Bournemouth train had come to a halt with the driver attempting to make contact with the Farnborough signalman. It was whilst stationary that the following Ilfracombe train struck the rear of the Bournemouth service at an estimated 20 mph resulting in the deaths of two passengers and 22 others (including the crew of No 453) requiring treatment for various injuries. SCT does not appear to have attended the accident and whilst all four lines were initially blocked by debris, two were restored to use by 6.30 am the following day and a full service was restored by 12.30 pm. In short the accident occurred in consequence of a power failure and in accordance with instructions the driver of the Bournemouth train, proceeding as instructed by the signalmen, stopping as instructed west of Farnborough. Here he attempted to contact the Farnborough signalman by telephone. Meaning the following Ilfracombe train was also proceeding under caution and although the crew stated they noticed the red light of the stationary train ahead both men confirmed they were used to seeing a red light of a train on what would normally be the local line and it was only at the last minute they realised the red light they were seeing applied to the stationary train immediately ahead. Under the circumstances the crew of the Ilfracombe train were exonerated in both the subsequent Ministry of Transport enquiry and at the Coroner's Inquest, with the basic cause down to the failure of the signalmen and their (in)action to resort to instructions in how to deal with this type of failure. (See http://www.railwaysarchive.co.uk/documents/MoT_Farnborough1947.pdf) In the three views here we see No 453 *King Arthur* having been recovered and standing at Eastleigh awaiting works repair.

Next time in this feature: More on the Eastleigh scrap line, new members of the 'USA' class, No 784 fitted with an experimental spark arrester chimney, Guildford turntable, flat-bottom track, a 'Z' shunting, restoring No 563 and a Royal special at Southampton Docks. *(Providing it all fits!)*

A taster of things to come with a view of the scrap line at Eastleigh probably around late 1947 or very early 1948. We see the last Adams 'T6' 4-4-0 class to remain in service, No 658, awaiting its fate – which was to come at Dinton in February 1948. This engine had originally been withdrawn in March 1939 but was reprieved along with sister engine No 659; the following month they were repaired at Eastleigh and subsequently put to work from the same shed. No 659, along with other survivors 664 and 666 from this once ten-strong class, was finally withdrawn in 1943 but No 658 managed to survive until December 1946 and when photographed had already been out of use for a year. In a life of 51 years it ran a recorded 1.33 million miles.

Rebuilt
The Letters and Comments pages

Not of the best quality but certainly interesting for what it is! The unique Bulleid 0-6-0 diesel shunter No 11001 'on its travels'. The exact location and date are not confirmed (I suspect somebody will identify it from the starting signal and calling-on arm) whilst from the headcode we are between Caterham and Purley. *Stephenson Locomotive Society*

A considerable offering this time and with grateful thanks to all. Hence without further ado we launch straight in and in no particular subject order, although we have tried to group comments on the same topic all together.

Firstly from Greg Beecroft on the subjects of **Tunnels SW44**; "Hello Kevin, I was on BR's Works Maintenance Committee when we reviewed the standards for examination of structures. With different requirements for bridges and tunnels there needed to be a clear definition of what comprised a tunnel. It was quickly realised that the railway needed two definitions of a tunnel, one for engineering management and the other for operating purposes, including observance of the rule book. The dictionary definition that you quote in SW44 is spot on for an engineer's definition of a tunnel. It is a structure with overburden. Operators are more concerned with the length of a tunnel and the fact that it is a dark area with limited space around the train. Even back in Southern Railway days there seems to have been no consistency as to what was a tunnel from an operator's point of view. St Cross Tunnel is clearly a bridge from a structural point of view. Originally it was a brick arch square on to the railway, with a road passing above it at an acute angle. In recent years it has been reconstructed as a concrete bridge, with much greater clearances, so it is now even harder to regard it as a tunnel. Conversely, structures I have long considered should be treated as tunnels for operating purposes, but are not, are the bridges that carry the Kensington and Ludgate lines from Longhedge Junction under the Brighton, Bournemouth and Windsor lines. These pass below thirteen tracks, so the enclosed area is sufficiently long for it to be prudent to apply the rule book requirements for tunnels. Incidentally, the engineering definition of a tunnel can result in a very short structure. The Moutier Tunnels in Switzerland are just eleven, eight and seven metres long, where the railway passes through rock outcrops."

Continuing on the same theme of **tunnels (and also later timetables)** from Nick Stanbury. "The interesting article on 'Southern Tunnels' (SW44) poses a number of questions and highlights some anomalies. First, it would seem that the Southern, at least, ignored the conventional definition of a tunnel as being 'dug' (or bored) as it seemed to regard anything that enclosed the railway (other than an obvious bridge or station roof) as being a tunnel. The well-known 'covered way' of 417yds at Cane Hill (Coulsdon) is a case in point, built as 'cut and cover' (although its roof was removed in the 1950s). Fulwell Tunnel (62yds: between Fulwell and Hampton) is another; its general appearance being that of a twin-arch skew bridge under a road. The position gets even murkier when two 'dive-unders' are considered: those at (New) Malden (50yds) and Byfleet (51yds), both of which are listed as tunnels in the SR 1934 General Appendix.

Whilst the 'Atlas of the Southern Railway' lists 153 (not 170) tunnels, they do not correspond exactly with the 153 listed in the GA. The Atlas, for example, includes that on the approach to Ramsgate Harbour (closed 1926), and the GA includes Mutley (on the GW main line east of Plymouth). Although the article suggests 62yds as the shortest length to qualify as an SR tunnel, the shortest listed as such in the GA are three each of 48yds: 'Canal Aqueduct' (between Brookwood and Farnborough); Cattedown (Plymouth Friary and Cattewater); and East Grinstead No. 2 (East Grinstead and Forest Row), of which the first (arguably a bridge?) does not appear in the Atlas. The article implies that the longest SR tunnel is Lydden (2,369yds) but suggests that this length is disputed, although as stated in both the GA and the Atlas. (The article also lists this tunnel as 'Shepherds Well' – a duplication.) It is not the longest; both sources agree that this is Sevenoaks tunnel at 3,453yds – not 3,520yds as stated in the article. As described in the article, there was originally one tunnel between Higham and Strood, subsequently divided into two with 66yds between them. For the record, Higham tunnel is 1,531yds and Strood tunnel is 2,329yds.

Turning briefly to Southern Region public timetables, Richard Simmons is correct to state (SW44) that there was a separate 'suburban' timetable for the London area. This was issued periodically through most of the 1950s and 60s and, living in Middlesex, was sufficient for my needs until I started venturing further afield in the mid-60s, at which time the separate divisional timetables were acquired. I recall that one issue of the latter had a truncated validity (possibly due to the wholesale alterations effective July 1967) and had to be replaced prematurely rather than just supplemented. Its successor was issued free-of-charge on surrender of the cover of the obsolete edition – the remainder of which I naturally kept 'for the archive' (and probably still have somewhere in storage!)."

Where steam once dwelt….the former steam shed at Brighton, no longer the home of 'C2X's, 'I3's, 'Atlantics' and 'Bulleids', now all is quiet. Steam has gone and will never return. (But as a blatant plug, do look out for the latest 'SW Special' on that very subject, 'Steam around Brighton' [actually '1950s Steam to Brighton'].)

Now from Richard Darkins reference **'Greenwich Park Revisited' in SW42**, "...I would like to correct the item on p82. The 'temporary bridge' built over the main line in 1958 has not been replaced – it remains to this day! All that happened in 2017 was that the original metal supports to the bridge were showing signs of rusting and most of them have now been encased in concrete. It will be a very disruptive project when it is eventually replaced, as there is no road access, with tracks both under and over which will need to be blocked for some considerable time – hence the need to patch it up as much as possible."

From Bruce Duncan on 'Salisbury – Exeter' (SW45): "Dear Kevin, I note in the editorial to number 44, you make a reference to the Salisbury to Exeter singling, and I am really looking forward to that event!

You will see that the after effect of such leaves us a huge problem today. It is not just the singling but with a modern successful railway, finding the finance to put back track and infrastructure and indeed get the DFT and TOC to renew old rolling stock (30 year old failing 159s) is a real problem, all with the background of a railway with little leadership, and a TOC apparently in difficulty and NR with no money. Oh if the line had been retained in its full effect.

I have attached our newsletter (No 6); although out of date by now (August 2018), it gives you the feeling of what we are doing and our web site also at www.serug.co.uk . (This is the 'Salisbury, Exeter Rail Users Group' and well worth a visit to their site – Ed.)

Keep up the good work with SW, it is a great read, and for me going to school in Guildford from the Guildford/Horsham line No 44 is perfect and Sidmouth too!"

An apology now from the editor as I have been rightly chastised by Roger McDonald. "It was good to see a picture of **41313 on the rear cover of SW44**, but I think the caption needs amendment. 41313 is still very much alive and with us; as I was purchasing my copy of SW in the shop at Havenstreet she passed by on a train!"

A once known sight but of course consigned to memory for close on 30 years... Having passed the building many times I often wondered what it was like inside but never had the chance. Fortunately the excellent 'BTF' production 'Terminus', which I am sure will be familiar to many, affords a glimpse at what we miss.

Now from Vic Freemantle concerning **accidents and SW43/44**. "I felt I had to advise the following re item in SW 43 p87/88 on 1901 railway accident, and your end note.

Even today the Coroner has in law extremely more investigative power, and is able to call witnesses, direct and control, etc., over such matters than the RAIB/ORR. He alone often directs or advises if any further investigation is required into sudden or unexplained deaths, such as these.

The following precis of another railway accident may help clarify this. Reginald Victor GEAR (my Grandfather), Platelayer, killed by light loco Wednesday 9 December 1953, whilst working in the ten foot between the up/down main lines, Eastleigh to Shawford.

He and another were killed by a passing light engine on the line at Brambridge, between Otterbourne junction and the Waterworks. They were struck by a light engine on what is (at that location) a four-track main line shortly after a train on the up local line had left swirling smoke in fading light and misty weather. The Coroner was present with a Jury at the inquest. Also present were representatives of the British Transport Commission, NUR and ASLEF, but none was called upon to speak. Evidence was given by a Station Foreman called to the scene. The above was reported in the local *Southern Daily Echo* the following

day with the inquest clearly adjourned as the final session was on 17 December, the coroner in the meanwhile asking about any warning equipment that might have been available. From this it will be seen that no actual separate Railway investigation was undertaken." (*Vic – thank you – of course, an altogether tragic and unfortunately common accident. The point I was likely trying to make and indeed have repeated since is that whilst I accept where a fatality occurs either the Coroner or BofT would be involved, it is when an accident occurred resulting in a derailment, or other failure and there were perhaps only just injuries – if at all – that resulted. These we know were the subject of internal reports. Reports also that do not seem to have survived to pass to the NRM or National Archives. Probably many were simply thrown out, but some surely must have been saved – Ed.*)

The subject of the big **diesels (SW44)** on the Southern Region in the early 1950s prompted this telephone call from Dave Smith, ex-Cove Models. Readers may recall I commented that we had no evidence that either the original SR pair or the LMS twins ever worked in multiple on the SR – but it certainly now appears that at least the latter two did! "Spotting at Woking late one July evening in 1952/3, Nos 10000 and 10001 came into together from the direction of Waterloo and crossed over to the slow line stopping in the down local platform. They were

Below and opposite: **Manual labour dealing with a landslip near to Blackheath station reportedly in August 1958. The time of year might seem a little strange for such an occurrence, although a glance at the meteorological reports for July and August of that year reveal 'the disturbed cyclonic weather of late July continued throughout August with a good deal of cloud and rain.' A 'W' class 2-6-4T is at the head of this engineer's train.** *J Hills*

at the head of a non passenger train of parcel type vans so this may have been test, ecs or simply a method of moving the two together to prevent a separate light engine movement."

Continuing on the same subject, this from John Davenport (some of whose original images appear in the article referred to). "No 10202 was a regular performer on the

10:54 Waterloo to Salisbury, fast to Woking then slow line." Turning now **to p39 of SW44** John adds, "Townroe photos – the 'T14' is approaching Woking and will shortly switch to the local line so probably the 10:54 again. (SCT had moved round from the casualties in the carriage siding.) Finally on p45 of the same issue, the 'Belle' is definitely stopped on the slow line platform at (West) Byfleet – the subway roof gives it away."

From Chris Longley, re the illustration on **p66 of SW44**. "The image is actually taken from the Templecombe end of the down (southbound) platform at Sturminster Newton. Not sure about the train but the June 1950 WTT shows a possible candidate: Train '236', 9.45 SO Bournemouth West – Manchester London Road, booked to run through at 10.34 whilst train '555', 8.20 Bristol TM -Bournemouth, called from 10.33 – 10.36. The leading carriage, M5498M, would be what appears to be an ex LMS Dia 1851 BTK from Lot 692 of 1933. Now for the locomotive, probably one of the group allocated to Bath from Spring 1951: 34040-43."

From Martin Upward, "I do not know if you remember me (be assured I do and all for the right reasons) with some additional detail as to **locations in SW44.** Pages 40 and 41: the divided 4 Cor unit is berthed in the Down sidings at Woking, London end of the station next to The Orphanage. Page 44 -The inaugural run of the restored Bournemouth Belle is taken from Woking Up Yard and the train is on the Down Fast Line at Woking Junction."

Next from Alan Moon with a **question on Mr Stroudley's 'Terriers'**. Hopefully a knowledgeable reader may be able to assist. "I wonder if anyone you know can help me with a query I have regarding Stroudley's Terriers. As you may recall, I have known these engines since 1957 (50+ years!) as I grew up near Lewes and learnt to swim at Newhaven close to the West breakwater (I do not think you can swim there now!).

I am trying to find out more about the cab roofs, of which there seems to be a degree of doubt. The original works drawings imply that the roof curves down to join the gutter in a concave curve, whereas a number of photographs...and the Dapol models...join a convex curve to a flat gutter. A friend who has looked at *Fenchurch* tells me that the roof is largely original. What I think has happened is that as the edges corroded over time, the domed shape was cut back and welded/rivetted to a flat 'gutter' piece up the edge angle.

I am in correspondence with Eric Gates of the Brighton Circle about this, also the NRM, but wondered if your photographic collection might have photographs of any of the domed cab roofs? Some photographs from the side do appear to show a much more bulbous dome shape than others. *(We have looked in our own archives but without certain confirmation – Ed.)*

As you will realise, we look down on our models more than the actual engines and I do not think Dapol's representation of the cab roof is a proper representation other than that of a preserved example. I think they used an IoW example for research for the 7mm one but it appears to be very similar to their original 4mm version currently now with Hornby. It will be interesting to see what the proposed new 4mm example is like, but I am not hopeful, particularly if they try to represent *Boxhill*!"

From Bill Allen on the apparent **paucity of EMU images, SW44**. "Your article on SR EMUs is quite correct in assuming the rarity of images. We were all so keen to record the remaining steam on the SR network that we ignored EMUs. Their approaching vintage and obsolescence was obvious and already in the 50s elderly 4SUBs formed of ex-steam stock were being withdrawn. 2NOLs, the notorious 'non lavatory' stock, occasionally appeared on the South Coast services, but the express units we used to transport us from Bognor and Chichester to Portsmouth, Brighton and London we took for granted. The ride of the 6PULs and 6PANs used on the Brighton and Eastbourne services was very rough but we in West Sussex were more privileged in having 12 coach formations from Barnham to London Victoria via Dorking North and Sutton. A 4COR and 4BUF from Bognor met and joined a single 4COR unit from Portsmouth Harbour. Equivalent trains ran from Portsmouth to London Waterloo via the 'Portsmouth Direct' using 4CORs and a full refreshment car on 4RESs. From Bognor the 7.4am departure was the 'commuter' train and woe betide a mere mortal if you sat in one of the seats that the regular card school used on their trip! Arrival in Victoria was 8.34am in time to get to the office. The returning 'commuters' caught the 5.29pm arriving back in Bognor at 7.3pm – a long twelve hour day!

But apart from reminiscing, the main object of my letter is to share a photo taken by my father, Ron, in the summer of 1938 depicting the first electric train into Bognor. The ceremonial opening of the conversion to electric traction of the Mid-Sussex and Sussex coast lines was on 30 June with inauguration of regular services on 2 July. The train is seen approaching Highfield Road bridge (still extant) to the obvious interest of workers and locals alike. Quite who and why there is a man between the tracks on the up line is unknown. In the background a standard SR Concrete bridge spans the tracks, presumably replacing a right of way footpath across the track, which the electrified third rail would have made a dangerous crossing.

The units are two 2 BILS (numbers undecipherable) without a headcode but occupied as illustrated by the individual looking out of a window, it may well have been a trial working."

Now from Mark Brinton, reference **Part 8 of 'The Lost Archives of Stephen Townroe' (SW43)**. "I liked the four pictures he took at Ryde Pier Head. Presumably these were taken during the summer of 1946? *(The latter is very possible as the negatives in this sequence cover the period July 1946 to May 1947 – Ed.)* If Stephen was Shed Master at Eastleigh at this time, then he would also have been responsible for both Ryde and Newport loco sheds. It is possible that he could have been on his way to a meeting with George Gardiner (Assistant for the IOW) at Newport who was responsible for the day-to-day management of both loco sheds. Hence the interest in No.15 which is at the head of a Newport & Cowes service.

Then flipping back to P37 and the picture of the steam hauled EMU at Allbrook, my first thought was that it was a stock delivery train from Eastleigh Carriage Works to London, probably Selhurst. The odd consist could be due to the need to have vehicles with conventional buffers and coupling hooks of the outer (cab) ends to attach the loco and brake van. EMU driving vehicles of the type featured had retractable side buffers with drop head automatic couplers at the cab end and three link coupling with centre buffer at the non-cab end. Vehicles two and three in the train are SUB/EPB intermediate coaches which would have single buffer and three link couplings at both ends. To avoid the need for match wagons when moving these vehicles, it would be usual (certainly in the 1970s-80s and probably then as well) to split a unit and put the additional vehicles in the middle for moves between depots/works. If this

Left: **The first electric unit arriving at Bognor.** *Bill Allen*

Opposite: **Behind the scenes at West Croydon.**

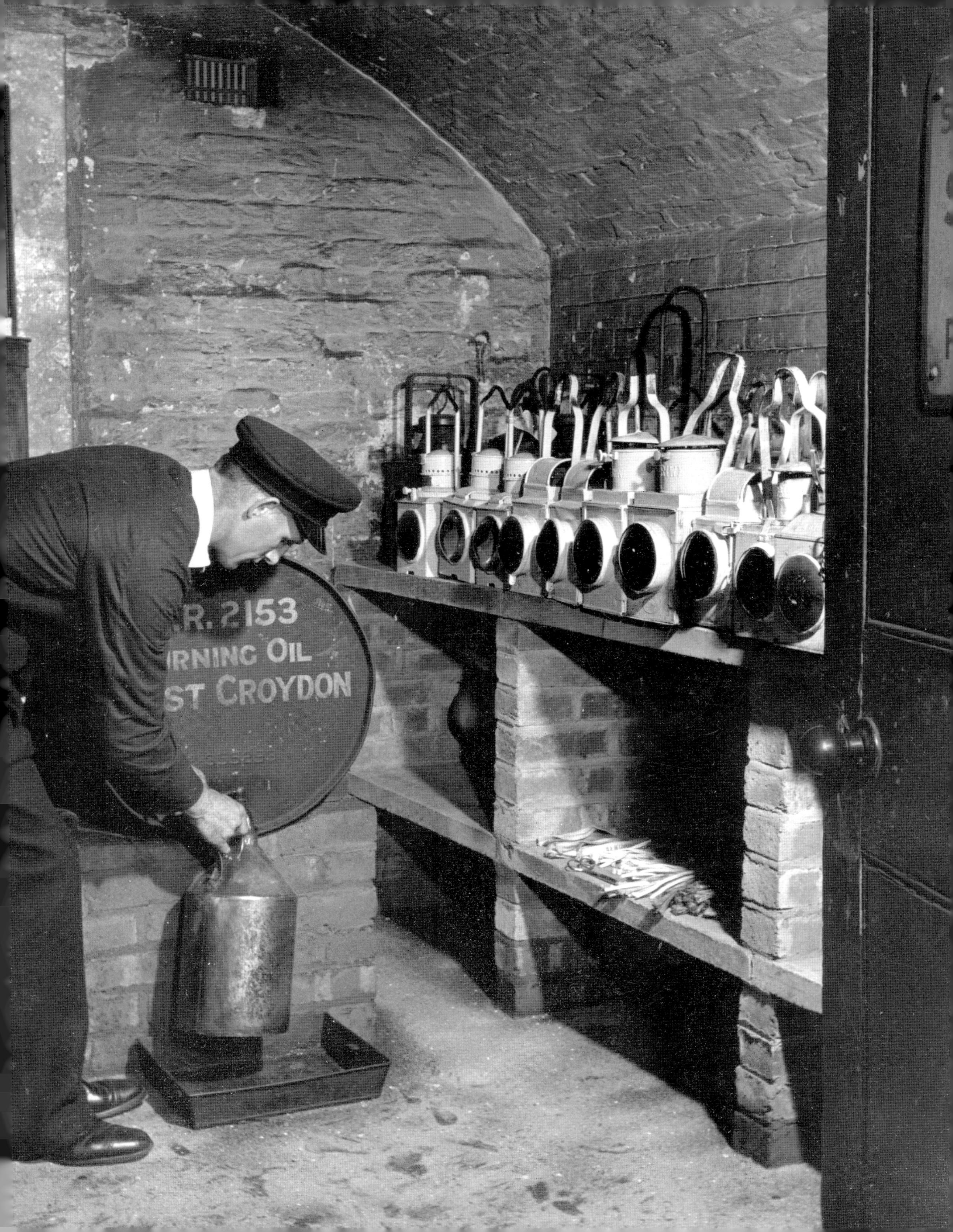
R. 2153
RNING OIL
ST CROYDON

were the case then I would have expected the fourth vehicle either to be a driving trailer or an intermediate trailer of the same unit as the leading coach. However the fourth vehicle in the train has what appears to be a crest on the side indicating that it is a motor coach. Alternatively the train could actually be the delivery of 4EPB unit 5302 which according to 'Southern Electric Vol.2' by David Brown had new BR design 1957 equipment motor coaches and SR designed trailer coaches and was delivered in 1961. This formation would match what I can make out of the first four vehicles in the train and would account for why the fourth vehicle in the train is another motor coach. The reference to 2HAP 6161 could refer to the last two carriages in the formation. The leading motor coach in the train certainly does not come from 6161 as this was delivered with a Commonwealth trailer bogie at the non-cab end and the vehicle in the picture has an earlier leaf sprung trailer bogie. David Brown suggests that the batch of vehicles which included unit 6161 was not delivered until 1962-3 though, which is too late for the photo, if the date is correct.

I did also spot your deliberate error in the caption of the photo on Page 5, presumably you were just testing the readers to see if we were paying attention! If the picture is at Millbrook then the line in the foreground would be the link to the north end of the New (Western) Docks not the Fawley branch."

Finally from Alan Postlethwaite a poem entitled 'Southern Soliloquy' inspired by reading Dylan Thomas.

"The Southern way with Southern rail
On Southern ballast all the while;
Southern engines, Southern trains,
What were the Southern's great domains?
South Eastern and Chatham o'er the Downs,
Through orchards, hop fields, Kentish towns;
To Dover, Folkestone, Queenborough too,
And Port Victoria, Hundred of Hoo.
London, Brighton and South Coast thrill
To seaside, dockside, Streatham Hill;
Sussex and Surrey, a great triangle,
Bluebell and Cuckoo stand out in the tangle.
Bold South Western to major ports:
Plymouth, Southampton and many resorts;
Exeter, Winchester, Basingstoke too,
Swiftly connected to Waterloo.
Knackered together in World War One,
Grouped in the Act of 1921;
So how did they fare, I hear you say?
Read all about it – The Southern Way."
(I feel somewhat speechless, but also grateful – Ed.)

The Last Steam Train to Exeter Central

Les Price

Rather befittingly, Saturday 8 January 1966 dawned grey and gloomy, somewhat appropriate as well as a host of mourners descended on Waterloo to witness the last rites of steam on the old 'South Western' main line to Exeter. I was just one of them.

'The Last Steam Train to Exeter Central' was a private charter organised by D. W. Winkworth and G. F. Bloxham with a view, no doubt, to recording a fitting tribute by the locomotives involved and so mark the passing of steam on the route. A very carefully considered choice of motive power had also been made in using two 'West Country' Pacifics, one, No. 34001 *Exeter* rebuilt in 1957 and the other No. 34015 *Exmouth* the latter still in its original condition, but both synonymous with the route. Conveniently each was also strategically placed, the former at Nine Elms and the latter at Salisbury.

As the participants assembled, *Exeter* backed slowly up from Nine Elms on to her train. She looked in 'good nick' and still sported both her nameplates. At 9.20 am the guard's whistle sounded and we set off. After skipping past her home

A grey day at Salisbury. No 34001 *Exeter* has just arrived from Waterloo (via Farlington, Fareham and Eastleigh) and will shortly be replaced by No 34015 *Exmouth* for the hoped for sprint to Exeter. *All images by the Author*

shed with a blast of the whistle, she eased to the curve through Clapham Junction before opening up for a canter through the south-west London suburbs and the Surrey stockbroker belt. At Woking, and in best rail tour tradition, we diverted off our westbound course and instead followed the Portsmouth direct line through Guildford, passing the latter platforms on time at 9.56 am, a schedule of thirty-six minutes for the thirty miles covered.

Having traversed the 'Portsmouth Direct', at Farlington Junction we bore right on to what is effectively the Portsmouth avoiding curve to our first stop at Fareham in order that *Exeter* could take on water. During the six minute stop, an enthusiastic throng were all over the tracks, taking photographs from every available vantage point. Despite this, we were only one minute late getting away. Interesting how the discipline of its day worked.

From Fareham we followed the original 'South-Western' Portsmouth route from Waterloo up to Eastleigh and then through the heart of 'Heavenly Hampshire' up the Test Valley past Romsey, Dunbridge and Dean before stopping at Salisbury. An hour's pause was planned here to allow *Exeter* to be relieved by 34015 *Exmouth*. As a Salisbury (72E) based engine she was obviously familiar with the 'South-Western' main line to the West Country.

Steam and diesel alongside each other at Salisbury shed, Nos 76016 (left) and 76008. Aside from the pair of 'Cromptons' there was also a 204hp 0-6-0 shunter lurking inside the depot.

There was also just enough time to make a dash to the shed and there outside, we found two engines in steam: a pair of Standard Class 4 2-6-0s Nos. 76016 and 76008. The former was sporting an Eastleigh (70D) shed code so must have been familiar with the route we had just travelled. The other was not bearing a shed code plate but was a Bournemouth (71B) based locomotive when it was withdrawn fourteen months later.

The schedule now allowed eighty-seven minutes for the eighty-eight miles outward trip to Exeter Central, a fraction more than a mile-a-minute start to stop. We left Salisbury promptly at 12.43pm, but it was a sluggish departure and we continued to lose time, already two minutes late at Wilton South, five by Gillingham and nine down by Yeovil Junction.

For the last half of the journey west *Exmouth* managed to hold her own against the clock; and we eventually arrived at Exeter Central just over nine minutes late at nearly 2.20 pm. But she still had steam to spare on arrival, witness her safety valve blowing; perhaps the delays were operational rather than down to the locomotive's performance?

Right and opposite: No 34015 *Exmouth* suitably adorned with white paint (as was customary on a number of specials country-wide in the final days of steam) seen awaiting departure from Salisbury.

Arrival at Exeter Central – 'nine down'. No 34015 certainly had a good batch of coal leaving Salisbury and shortly after this view was taken the safety valves started to lift. Steam engines were strange creatures and it was not unknown for one to behave perfectly and make as much steam and more as was required with the regulator closed and yet perform poorly under load conditions.

Above and opposite: **Preparing for departure from Exeter with the art-deco style platform lights showing up well in the gloom of a January afternoon. In the first of the views the fireman appears to be attempting to secure the smokebox door – had it been drawing air and might this have even been the cause of *Exmouth*'s disappointing performance on the way down?**

Exmouth then came off the train and departed light to Exmouth Junction shed for servicing and turning whilst we, the passengers, had two hours to spend at Exeter. Exmouth Junction (72A) had officially closed to steam on 31 May 1965 but happily still had the facilities to service and turn locomotives.

By the time *Exmouth* reappeared at Central Station it was late afternoon and the light was fading fast. Amid the gloom, the ex- Southern Railway electric platform lamps stood out like beacons lighting the mournful crowd absorbing the melancholy of the moment. On time at 4.25 pm we were away again. For the return journey the time had been set at 96 minutes for the eighty-eight miles 'Up' leg back to Salisbury. Unfortunately though, even this easier schedule was beyond the capabilities of No 34015. Passing Sidmouth Junction we were five minutes behind time, by Axminster it was eight minutes and through Yeovil Junction eleven and so it continued, until we rolled into Salisbury thirteen minutes late.

By now it was also pitch black, the darkness only being illuminated by Salisbury's platform lamps. *Exmouth* was relieved here by *Exeter* now fully rested and refreshed for her run back home to Waterloo. Smart station work meant we were able to regain three minutes and so departed just 'ten

down' at 6.11 pm against a booked time of 6.01 pm. Eighty-eight minutes had been allowed to cover the eighty-four miles to Waterloo with many of us hoping this would indeed be achieved with a mile a minute timing. It was not to be and by Worting Junction we had dropped two minutes but to the credit of the engine and her crew thereafter we kept schedule and arrived at Waterloo just eleven minutes late, covering the last fifty miles in fifty-five minutes.

So it was not to be. There was no crowning glory on the 'South-Western' main line. The days of the 'ACE' were not to be relived. The die-hards who wanted one last exhilarating run on the old main were denied. And the rest of us went home dejected that it was all over. Personally it was my only trip behind steam over the route from Salisbury to Exeter and sadly I had never experienced the type of journey known by John Betjeman and other exalted company on the 'ACE' to Cornwall.

And of *Exeter* and *Exmouth*? Both remained in service until the end of steam operations on the Southern; *Exeter* at Nine Elms and *Exmouth* at Salisbury with the former operational until July and the latter succumbing slightly earlier in April 1967. They may well have met again; on the scrap lines of Messrs. Cashmore at Newport where both were destined to be dismantled.

Ambulance Trains at Basingstoke in WW2

John Springer

(Articles that appear in 'SW' can sometimes come via a convoluted route. Such is the case here with this piece, which first appeared in the newsletter of the 'Aldershot & District Bus Interest Group'. As an example of a little bit of detective work worth pursuing, readers may find it interesting how it came to be published...

In late July 2018 I received a note from 'SW' reader John Busby alerting me to the article in question and for the simple reason the 'Aldershot' article contained references to Ambulance Trains – a topic we had recently covered in 'SW42'. The piece John alerted me to was based specifically on personal reminiscences featuring such a train that was dealt with at Basingstoke in WW2 and whilst geographically the earlier 'SW42' Ambulance Train article dealt mainly with the SECR, the content of the new piece was, I considered, so interesting it was worth attempting to secure permission for it to be seen by those

with a 'railway leaning'. There followed further correspondence with John Busby who in turn put me in touch with Les Smith, the editor of the 'Aldershot' newsletter, and whilst he was only too willing to help, it was rightly pointed out that I would need to seek out permission from the original writer, John Springer. Contact was duly made, and what followed was a series of phone calls and emails elaborating greatly on the original short piece with particular reference to railway operation both at Basingstoke and in the vicinity at that time in WW2. We found it fascinating as I am sure you will too. My grateful thanks to all those mentioned – ED. The article that follows has also been edited to include additional information provided by the original author in communication with SW.)

Above and opposite: **Basingstoke down yard, road access to which was via a gap at the west end of the down side station buildings.**

I n 1940 I became a member of Basingstoke Division St John Ambulance Brigade Ambulance Cadet Corps ('Ambulance Cadet' also meant male only at that time). Having been an active participant in the Corps, two years later I recall getting home from school one day in late 1942 to be told the police had called at my home and that my services were required the next night. I had been directed to join eight or nine other boys of my age at Basingstoke's Southern Railway Goods Yard at 01.30 next morning to be ready to help unload 400 stretcher cases from an Ambulance train. The patients were to be loaded into ambulances to be taken to Park Prewett Hospital EMS (Emergency Medical Service*).

I walked up to the yard in the blackout to where about six old road coaches with their backs replaced with a type of canvas flap were waiting. The seats had also been replaced by sets of grooved wooden runners to take the standard 'Furley' stretchers at a low level, and another runner at window sill level to take an upper stretcher. There were 'strap – hanging' loops for the outer edges. We had to blanket (as was stipulated in contemporary St John's manuals) and stack all the stretchers

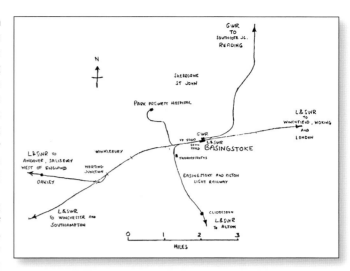

Basingstoke area map, obviously for 'LSWR' read 'SR'. By the time of this article the Alton line had closed and only ventured as far as a siding serving the Thornycroft works. Micheldever, which is also mentioned in the text, is the first station south of Basingstoke en-route to Winchester.

* Park Prewett Hospital on the outskirts of Basingstoke had been built to house psychiatric patients and by the end of August 1939, some 1,400 were resident. All but 80 were moved out by this time to varying locations from Wales, to Gloucester, Wiltshire and Hampshire. Park Prewett was now designated as a casualty clearing station as well as providing 2,000 beds for both civilian and service casualties away from what were considered to be high-risk enemy targets.

on each vehicle before the train arrived. I think that at least three of these vehicles were Strachan-bodied vehicles. The half cab vehicles loaded 12 stretchers – loading order being – bottom front left – bottom right front – upper left front – upper right front. The coach style vehicles only loaded ten because of the driver's space.

Promptly at 01.30 a shunter waved a reversing train into the yard and all the lights came on – this despite the blackout. We helped pass our prepared stretchers into the back of the train and then rode with the ambulances to the front of the train. Train orderlies next started passing loaded stretchers out. It took six or eight boys to bring a man on a stretcher from train height down to loading level and put it into a road vehicle. As soon as a vehicle was loaded, one boy had to ride in the back – holding on somehow – as it drove the 3½ miles or so to Park Prewett. Illumination inside was with some blue-painted light bulbs. The drivers came from the ATS (Auxiliary Transport Service). Most of these ATS men were older reservists or unfit for active service. Although nowadays Basingstoke hospital – close by the former Park Prewett site – is accessed by modern well-lit roads, at the time it was almost like venturing into the country. The ATS vehicles were driving on unmarked country roads and with only one masked headlight on dip or two on full beam. Even on full beam these headlights were as dim as a TocH lamp! Arriving at the hospital, butchers'-aproned men lifted the canvas and sent the driver and boy into the kitchen. Here we were given a pint of cocoa and a huge corned-beef wad (sandwich), the sort of quantity normally provided for a family of four for a week. Having refreshed ourselves, the vehicle was ready to return, during which time the boy's (my) duties were to blanket and stack all his stretchers once more before the vehicle arrived back at one end

of the train and the process was repeated. This type of call-out operation continued at intervals until late 1945 or very early 1946.

By the time 'VJ Day' was declared at about 00.30 on 14 Aug 1945, we were at camp with our great friends from the Totton Boys Brigade at Gurnard, Isle of Wight. I also recall that also around this time and for a while after, we had had the task of unloading injured returning Japanese POWs. That was not an easy job for us for despite being older and physically grown, manoeuvring a man on a stretcher in a confined space was not easy.

What I recall most of about those sad days was the way some of the injured men reacted to us. They were absolutely terrified no matter what was said by us or others in an attempt to reassure them. I quickly learnt it was our grey uniforms that were the problem – the Japanese too had work-grey uniforms and it was the connection with this colour that was causing some of the men to have what must have been flashbacks over the treatment they had perhaps personally experienced and no doubt witnessed as well.

As if to prove how it can justifiably be called a small world sometimes, I recall speaking to a group in Yorkshire about my experience of 50 years with St John's. Afterwards one of the audience approached me and told me that he had almost certainly been driving on at least one of the times I was loading and/or riding.

Part of the former GWR station at Basingstoke with the public house of the same name just visible behind. The view is included to show a WW2 Nissan type hut that was erected on the platform of the former GWR station. Originally the GWR station possessed an overall roof. In the foreground the single line of rails led around the rear of the SR Platform 4 and was a means of access to the locomotive shed without occupying any of the through lines.

Basingstoke shed in September 1954 playing host to locomotives involved in some of the special workings to the Farnborough Air Show, including visitors, No 251 from the GNR and 'D11' No 62663. In the right background is the Eli Lilly building surrounded as it was then by green fields.

(Rather than attempt to edit John's notes further, the other points made as clarification and expansion are listed below as simple notes. I am sure that like me the reader will find them interesting.)

John was not aware of any photograph taken showing the repatriation of wounded servicemen from the trains, not least as photography or filming was strictly controlled in what was a 'sensitive area' – see later. In 1942 air raids and incursions by lone enemy aircraft were still a very real threat when the first of the trains arrived. John is of the opinion there may well have been special air patrols of friendly craft activated when the potentially dangerous act of lighting a major goods yard and carrying out such a concentrated vehicle movement was taking place. In later years and despite the fact the government had published seemingly triumphal pictures of men having

been rescued from Japanese brutality, it is unlikely the authorities would have wanted to let the public see the poor demented individuals we were unloading: all still in dire need and this despite having received the best attention possible on their respective journeys back to 'blighty'.

The actual boat arrival and transfer times to Basingstoke were also no doubt heavily censored, and probably arranged on an 'as required' basis by Southampton Control or other control area.

In preparation also for 'D-Day', John also recounts that by 1943 Basingstoke was the last furthest station south to which ordinary travellers could venture without special permits.

The status of having a military exclusion zone beyond Basingstoke on the Southern Railway arose because of the sensitivity of the excavations around Micheldever tunnel and marshalling yards. It was at Micheldever that a number of massive underground fuel tanks had been cut into the hillside (out of use in the 21st century but still easily visible cut into the hillside north of the station). In addition there were underground works containing control rooms, bunkers and, crucially, massive fuel storage, with direct supply from Stanlow (Essex), all of which would later support and supply PLUTO.

John continued that the Basingstoke St John's could not even take our Cadet Band down to Totton by rail to join forces with their own Boys Brigade Band (the respective bandmasters were brothers) because one could not, unless properly accredited, buy a rail ticket to anywhere below Basingstoke on that line. He comments, "I do know that we did manage to get down to Totton by road by which there was no restriction." John states,"...it is possible that on through services train staff ensured that all window blinds were drawn when the train passed through Basingstoke."

(This in itself raises a number of questions. How was this restriction enforced, how indeed about those through bookings – as the guard or other person going through the train to pull down blinds would surely have aroused suspicion anyway. What about persons living or genuinely having need to visit others in the prohibited area? It appears there were no, or only limited, restrictions on other routes to Southampton from Newbury, Andover, Salisbury, via Alton, Guildford, etc., although another source [Harold Gasson] recounts the whole of the south was 'restricted', certainly there was a considerable build-up of men and equipment in places like the Winchester by-pass and on the common at Southampton, the former certainly easily visible from a passing train coming south from Newbury. This would appear to be a topic on which there is little further information and readers' comments would be welcomed.)

Park Prewett was also where troops, in this case Canadians, were billeted. Nearby Eastrop Lane Drill Hall was used as an EMS for these men. In addition some of these men were on the Camrose Estate (better known as Hackwood Park south-east of the town) at the time owned by Lord Beaverbrook. Some of these Canadian troops had been involved in the abortive Dieppe raid and the later events at Slapton Sands.

Eastrop Lane Drill Hall was also a big NAAFI. At the time John lived in nearby Chequers Road and was very friendly with the son of the caretaker. He would often go down after their closing time (10.30 pm?) to help get the place cleaned and tidied ready for the next day. Many of the men using it also came from Bramley and some regularly escaped to take refuge in our house, known to them as 'Oddbod's Hall', for simple peace and quiet. Members of the Basingstoke Division of St John's, including John, also had the task of training troops in First Aid.

There was slight amusement recalled when the first American troops arrived at Basingstoke. They were detrained on the SR platform and then walked directly on to the GWR for parade on GWR land above the station near the railway stables. John recounts he was one of the boys observing this and howled with laughter as we watched them form up. The NCO came out with, to an English boy, ridiculous orders, "Forward" when he meant "Quick March" and the squelch – squelch – squelch of the GI's soft footwear compared with the more usual 'crash – crash – crash' of 'proper' boots.

One final point concerning Basingstoke is the Eli Lilly building seen from the railway by all trains approaching Basingstoke station from the west, and standing on the north side of the line. As built it was orientated very precisely, having its back to the little rural service road that is the Kingsclere Road. Constructed in 1935/6 it could, as mentioned, be seen by anyone travelling on the main line and which of course was then the main access to London for travellers having disembarked from the transatlantic liners at Southampton. The firm of Eli Lilly insisted that their building in one of the Southern States of the USA be virtually recreated at Basingstoke. As all the boat trains ran past the Eli Lilly Basingstoke site, American passengers would suddenly see the frontage and name display of one of the most iconic new buildings in The States. What a magnificent advertisement to homesick citizens, although unfortunately it later made a great aiming/navigation point for the Luftwaffe. (The structure still stands today although is no longer in commercial use. The intention is to turn it into 56 flats with a further 500 homes on the site.)

The Croydon, Oxted & East Grinstead Railway

Jeremy Clarke

Over-bridge between Lingfield and Dormans likely recorded when the railway was either still under construction or just complete. (A number of similar views of the newly completed Croydon, Oxted & East Grinstead Railway appear in an article in SW No 7.)

East Grinstead is a Wealden town of some 26,400 people and ancient enough to be recorded in the Domesday Book of 1086. It lies some thirty miles south of London and about 400' above sea level, standing almost four-square upon the meeting point of four counties, Surrey, Kent, East Sussex and West Sussex, though administratively it is now in the last to which it was transferred by boundary changes in 1974. It is ironic that much commercial and residential development has taken place in and around the town, now making it contiguous with Felbridge to the north-west, since its best-known commuter, Dr Richard Beeching, had years before set out his proposals for closing most of the railway routes serving it!

Likewise Oxted has an entry in Domesday, its Grade 1 listed church being Norman at the base. The town lies some nine miles south-east of Croydon, the original village, now Old Oxted, perched on the edge of the Eden valley, is about three-quarters of a mile from the station and the 'new' village that has arisen around it since the arrival of the railway. The population at the 2011 census was just over 11,000.

By the latter part of the 18th century East Grinstead had become an overnight stopping point for coaches between London and the South Coast counties of Kent and East Sussex, no fewer than twelve inns catering for travellers by 1781. After that date, traffic declined as the popularity of Brighton grew, travellers now passing to the west as did the London & Brighton Railway, opened throughout in September 1841. But the proximity of that line caused a Bill, promoted locally, to be brought before Parliament seeking authorisation for a branch from Three Bridges, the first of a quartet of routes that eventually served the town.

This line, or something rather like it, had first been proposed in 1845 as part of a much larger scheme to connect the major naval towns of Portsmouth, Chatham and Sheerness by rail. It involved co-operation between the LSWR, L&BR and SER and perhaps for that reason disagreements among the companies as to precise routeing and 'who did what', as well as division of funding, prevented a Bill being brought forward. The Brighton had anticipated building and working the section between Horsham and East Grinstead, though Parliament only authorised the 6½-mile long section eastwards from Three Bridges, and that in 1846. However, work did not proceed and it was left to the independent East Grinstead Railway Company to come up with fresh proposals in 1852. At the same time the EGR approached the Brighton to work the line on a 999-year lease at £2,000 pa. With the lease secure and the right reserved to the LBSCR to purchase the company within or after ten years, the East Grinstead Railway obtained Parliamentary approval. Following some delay due to late objections to part of the route by a local landowner, the line opened on 9 July 1855. Despite the start date, the Brighton did not take up the lease until 1858, or indeed purchase the line for another twenty years.

Copyhold Junction with a train from Horstead Keynes via Ardingly heading towards Haywards Heath.

The second line of the four was a continuation of the first, though built under the auspices of the East Grinstead, Groombridge & Tunbridge Wells Railway. This was in effect another portion of the grand and failed 'joining-up-the-navy' plan of 1845. The South Eastern Railway and the Brighton were bitter rivals over this part of the route though once it failed to materialise, the LBSCR set about making sure the South Eastern would not have any further opportunity to encroach. But once again promotion was local, incorporation and authorisation coming on 7 August 1862. With construction under way, suggestions were made that Hartfield on this line should be joined to Uckfield. Though this came to nothing it anticipated the later line to Uckfield from Groombridge. After a number of delays the railway opened on 1 October 1866, worked from the first by the LBSCR which had purchased it in 1864.

The third line arrived from the south. The Lewes & East Grinstead Railway had been promoted in 1875 by the Earl of Sheffield and other local landowners. Running north via Sheffield Park from Culver Junction on the aforementioned Lewes-Uckfield-Groombridge line which opened on 3 August 1868, this was seen by the Brighton as another buffer against any South Eastern ambitions. Great things were expected of the L&EGR following its authorisation on 10 August 1877, for it was built to take double track, though south of Horsted Keynes only single line ruled to the end. It opened on 1 August 1882 having been acquired by the LBSCR at an early stage of construction. (Horsted Keynes to Haywards Heath via Ardingly opened thirteen months later.)

Meanwhile things had also been moving to the north following the South Eastern's unsuccessful bid to make its main line to Tonbridge via Croydon, Oxted and Edenbridge. Having authorised the route, Parliament backtracked following sanction of the London & Brighton Railway in 1837, permission being withdrawn in the belief there would never be enough traffic to justify two routes running more or less parallel for the six miles between Penge and Purley. Instead the two companies were ordered to share the Brighton Line as far as Redhill, that being a convenient point for the South Eastern to strike east. In view of this the two made an agreement in 1848 that the area north of this SER line and east of the Brighton Line should be considered SER territory, the agreement being confirmed in 1864; the SER opening its Redhill to Tonbridge route in August 1842.

Oxted viaduct. This is one of several girder viaducts on this line. (See also the SEMG page at http://www.semgonline.com/structures/struct_57.html with images and information by Greg Beecroft.)

The Surrey & Sussex Junction Railway of 1865 followed a very similar proposal to that made the previous year by an apparently independent company, though there is some evidence it had the backing of a few LBSCR directors, including the then Chairman, Leo Schuster. By way of retaliation the SER had put forward a Bill for a line from Croydon to Eastbourne, but by mutual agreement the Bills for both were withdrawn before Parliamentary consideration.

The LBSCR-backed independent S&SJR remained in being however, and the S&SJR Bill, now with open Brighton backing, came again to Parliament, causing a furore as in South Eastern eyes it broke the 1848 agreement. The Brighton responded by pointing out the line was designed to join places already on its network and therefore could not be deemed as contravening the agreement. That may have been plausible in fact but it certainly broke the spirit of the agreement!

The S&SJR was authorised on 6 July 1865 to run from Croydon via Oxted to join the East Grinstead-Tunbridge Wells line (No. 2 above, then still under construction) at Groombridge. Further disputes followed, including South Eastern assertions some land purchases were illicit. This antagonism became so bitter the SER joined its great rival, the Chatham, in proposing a joint line between London and Brighton via Lewes. Though an Act was obtained for it, nothing further happened. However, construction of the S&SJR started immediately, the contractors, Messrs Waring, making brisk progress with many of the earthworks, including the Riddlesdown, Oxted and Limpsfield tunnels and two fine brick viaducts, being completed before serious financial problems beset the project. These arose mainly from the failure of the banking house of Overend, Gurney in June 1866.

That business had started out in 1800 as a Discount House in the name of Richardson, Overend & Co. This activity had generally been carried out by merchants as a sideline to their usual activities but by concentrating exclusively on the practice, O&G was an instant success and in time became the largest discounter in the world. Samuel Gurney, of the Norwich banking family, joined the firm in 1807 and took control of Overend, Gurney & Co two years later. But following his death in 1856 the business began to expand its portfolio, taking on long-term investments, railway stock among them, rather than remaining a leading discounter, a practice that required holding only short-term cash reserves. Overend, Gurney soon found itself with liabilities four times its assets and in an effort to retrieve the situation became incorporated in mid-1865, shares selling at a hefty premium that could only be justified by its reputation. But that did not save it as the value of stock and bond prices declined rapidly, railway shares among them, and credit became more difficult to obtain. An application to the Bank of England for financial assistance being refused, Overend, Gurney suspended payments in May 1866, its bankruptcy the following month bringing about the collapse of more than two hundred companies, including several banks. The repercussions of this fall out were also felt by a number of railway concerns including the mighty Great Western.

The Brighton was another of the companies affected though it escaped the bankruptcy that engulfed the Chatham, many of whose engines for some years thereafter could be seen bearing lead plates stating they were in pawn to certain creditors ; but with construction of the S&SJR underway at the time, the SER's simmering resentment boiled over. Lengthy and bitter negotiations failed to resolve matters resulting in the Duke of Richmond being called on to arbitrate. On his decision, an Act of Parliament in 1869 authorised the transfer of the S&SJR to the Brighton. But by this time, as already noted and because of expenditure elsewhere on some unprofitable lines, the LBSCR was itself in some financial difficulty. Its application to Parliament in 1870 to abandon was refused and a penalty of £50 per day for failure to complete the line imposed. The Brighton decided to cut its losses and pay £32,250, the maximum limit of the penalty, which in turn allowed the S&SJR powers to lapse.

There matters rested and might have remained so had a number of later schemes not been projected following a general financial recovery. Among these was a line from Caterham to Westerham via Godstone and Oxted, which actually obtained an Act in 1876, but the company was dissolved in 1880 without a sod being turned. Revival of the proposed SER route to Tonbridge via Oxted and Edenbridge, but this time starting from Caterham, was another that came to nothing. Another joint venture by the SER and LCDR in 1875 was for a line from Beckenham to Brighton by way of Warlingham, Godstone, East Grinstead, Lindfield and Clayton. The fact remained, however, that a line once promoted to serve most of these very places was already half-built and clearly provided the most convenient way forward.

With a change to the southern part of the original S&SJR route to an end-on junction at East Grinstead with the line proposed from Lewes, the Croydon, Oxted & East Grinstead Railway was authorised in 1878, agreement being reached that the portion between South Croydon and Crowhurst, where the SER Redhill-Tonbridge line crossed the new route, should be jointly owned by the Brighton and South Eastern. Joseph Firbank, the contractor for the Lewes & East Grinstead Railway, also tendered successfully for refurbishing the S&SJR's neglected works, completing the route in 1881. But already other connecting routes were in progress. The independent Woodside & South Croydon Railway had been authorised in 1880 to make a junction with the CO&EGR at Selsdon; it became another LBSCR/SER joint venture when purchased in 1882. The Oxted & Groombridge Railway – effectively the southern part of the original S&SJR scheme – got its Act in 1881 and was purchased by the LBSCR three years later, opening in 1888.

After the usual Board of Trade inspection the Croydon, Oxted & East Grinstead Railway came into use on 18 February 1884; East Grinstead's famed two-level station having been completed four months earlier. Double track throughout, the line begins at South Croydon Junction, 11 miles 29 chains from London Bridge and eight chains south of the station. This marks the start of an almost unbroken six-mile climb to a summit just short of Oxted tunnel, initially at 1 in 83 but mainly at 1 in 100. The now-closed and demolished station at Selsdon (much more accurately Selsdon Road until September 1935) stood only thirty chains from South Croydon, the main

Oxted tunnel, at 2,266 yards, located between Woldingham and Oxted.

buildings, in brick, being at the London end in the 'V' of the converging Woodside route, with the roofed footbridge to the Up platform close by. A subway gave access to the W&S platforms. The signal box stood at the country end of the station, opposite and controlling the junction with the Woodside line. ('North' box, on that line, closed in 1935, its duties taken over by 'South' box.). Selsdon itself lies almost two miles from the station site and about 300' higher.

There never was much passenger patronage here with the main Brighton line being so close. The station closed as a wartime economy measure on 1 January 1917, the Oxted line platforms reopening on 1 March 1919 though those serving the Woodside line had to wait for electrification in September 1935. The number of Oxted line trains calling subsequently declined almost to nothing during the 1950s and ceased entirely from 15 June 1959. The station saw its last passenger train on 13 May 1983 as a result of the closure of the Woodside line and though demolition followed, the Oxted line platforms remain, if in a sorry state.

Selsdon boasted a substantial goods yard of five lengthy sidings with connections at the northern end on the Woodside line. One of these led into a dock and, unusually, there was also a cattle dock here. The yard closed in October 1968 though the storage facilities set up there by the Anglo-American Oil Company in 1894 were not abandoned until just short of their centenary in 1993, access latterly being provided by a short stub of the W&SCR Down line retained after closure to provide a 'neck'. A small residential development now occupies the station site while limited commercial activity continues in the area of the goods yard.

Whyteleafe station looking north in 1952.

Just over a half-mile onward from Selsdon once stood Purley Downs Golf Club Halt. This was a private station which had opened in 1914 and closed in 1927. A precursor to many such small and remote halts of today, trains would call by request.

Sanderstead station, at 12m 23ch and on a very short piece of 1 in 376, opened with the line and had a goods yard of four sidings on the Up side, one of which led into a dock behind the platform. The lead-in was directly to the up line at the up end of the station. The yard here closed in March 1961. The station building, also on the Up side, was a standard SER timber weatherboard structure with a covered footbridge near its Up end. A quite pleasing chalet-style brick station building came into use in 1987 following a fire in the original and its subsequent demolition. The signal box stood part way along the Down platform; it closed in 1985 but was not demolished for another two years. Sanderstead is another station some 300' below its village though it is only about a mile distant.

The section of line between Selsdon and Sanderstead was electrified as part of the W&SR scheme, the third rail being laid in anticipation of electric trains from Woodside continuing

onward from a junction south of Sanderstead to serve the Surrey Heights Light Railway to Orpington. The SHLR had been proposed in 1925 and was authorised at the end of December 1928 under a Light Railway Order, with Col. H F Stephens named as engineer: the SR had agreed to electrify the line and work it, but the scheme was dropped following the monetary depression of the early-1930s, which meant the provision of the third rail mid-decade was a measure of optimism still felt about resurrection of the line. However, Green Belt Acts post-WW2 sadly put paid to this, although it could have been a very useful cross-country route. Oddly, this small section was the only piece of electrified track on the whole of the 'Oxted Group' of lines until conversion from South Croydon to East Grinstead in 1987. (The thirty chains between South Croydon and Selsdon had actually had third rail installed in 1984 following closure of the route from Woodside to permit some electric services to continue to terminate at Sanderstead.)

Riddlesdown was opened by the Southern Railway on 5 June 1927 in a bid to encourage housing development in its vicinity. That turned out to be rather an inauspicious time and little development had taken place before the war or, indeed,

East Grinstead High Level station with its four platform faces. It is this station, now simply renamed 'East Grinstead', that survives today, albeit in totally different form.

for some years after. The station stands at about the centre of a two mile-long 1 in 100 gradient and 13m 38ch from London Bridge. In 1957 the platforms and small, rather crude timber station buildings were reconstructed, the former in prefabricated Exmouth Junction concrete, the latter in brick, the main one being on the up side. At the same time electric lighting superseded the gas lamps on the platforms and in the building. Being at the point where high embankment and deep cutting meet, no goods yard was provided here but neither is there any means of passing between the platforms. Instead these are accessed by separate paths leading up from Lower Barn Road which the line bridges north of the station.

Ten chains further on and still climbing at 1 in 100, the line enters the 837-yard long Riddlesdown tunnel. This brings it out high up on the eastern flank of the Caterham Valley with the ex-SER Purley-Caterham branch in the valley bottom. Until June 1948 'Riddlesdown Intermediate' box stood eight chains beyond the tunnel's southern portal: there never was a signal box at the station itself. The box also marked the start of a half-mile of level track before the gradient resumes, now at 1 in 264, to cross a steel-girder viaduct spanning a quarry and cement works, for here we are well up on the chalk of the North Downs. This viaduct is typical of those built by the CO&EGR, the longer three of its five spans later being provided with intermediate supports to allow for heavier axle loads. The cement works nearby were never rail connected and ceased operation in 1969.

Upper Warlingham ('& Whyteleafe' between 1894 and 1900, 15m 33ch from London Bridge) is on a short piece of level track. It opened with the line and provides a birds-eye view of Whyteleafe station in the valley below. In reality 'Upper Warlingham' does not exist, the prefix being added soon after opening to distinguish it from 'Warlingham' station on the Caterham line. That station was renamed, with much greater accuracy, Whyteleafe South in 1956 but the anachronistic 'Upper' defining the Oxted line station remains. Like both Selsdon and Sanderstead, the village centre of Warlingham lies well above and about ¾-mile from the line although more recently housing development, particularly post-WW2, has covered much of the slope of the Caterham Valley down toward the station. The station's buildings are quite substantial, albeit with timber buildings, now rendered, the main one being on the Up side; the signal box stood off the southern end of the Up platform. Extensions to the once fully enclosed footbridge between the platforms give potential passengers as well as the general public access from the high ground east of the line directly to the station buildings and forecourt to the west. The bridge's roof and glazing were removed in 1956. The three sidings forming the goods yard lay behind the up platform with connections at the south end while a down side dock siding was at the London end of the station. This siding's head shunt had a 4½-tons capacity crane beside it. Goods facilities were withdrawn on 4 May 1964, the signal box going with the commissioning of Oxted Panel box in November 1985.

Whyteleafe Lime Works, immediately south of the station on the Down side, was provided with a private siding in 1886 but this was out of use before 1939, though production continued until the early 1960s. The 1 in 100 climb has resumed here and continues to the summit just north of Oxted tunnel but for a very short level stretch before Woldingham viaduct.

The Low Level station at East Grinstead which once served Bluebell Line trains.

Shortly before coming to this structure, which stands just beyond mp16½, are four arches in what are pleasantly weathered red brick, taking the railway into the Caterham valley after which it curves away southward. (The viaduct was one of the two built by Waring for the S&SJR more than a decade before the line opened.)

Woldingham station itself (17m 15ch) is the highest on the line, straddling the 450' contour. Opened in July 1885 as Marden Park but taking the present title nine years later, it's another that lies well below and a mile or more from the named village in a location which remains quite rural, a situation to which the down side SER weatherboard building seems eminently suited. In this exposed position, the shelter on the up platform is rather more substantial than usual but the footbridge, a Southern Railway version at the country end, is another that had its roof and glazing removed some years ago, in this case in 1960.

The goods yard, of two sidings, was on the Down side behind the platform and made its connection into the down line at the south end almost opposite the signal box. It was an early closure, in May 1959, though engineers continued to use the dock siding behind the platform for some years. One of the Covenants under which land for the station was acquired was that there should be no means by which 'strong drink' could be provided, so no 'Railway Inn' or 'Station Hotel' graces the forecourt or approach.

Because there is no easing of the gradient, 'catch points' were installed in the down line some 11 chains to the north, though following closure of the yard, which meant loose-coupled freight trains no longer shunted here, these were removed.

The summit of the route is at a short level 17m 45ch from London Bridge. Twenty-one chains further on, and on a gradient that falls for almost nine miles, initially at 1 in 132, the line plunges into Oxted tunnel. This is another S&SJR-built structure driven through the chalk of the North Downs and unusual in that it curves gently toward the east throughout its length on a radius of about one mile. At 2,261 yards it has the distinction of being the longest tunnel on the former LBSCR, two yards longer than that at Clayton.

A quarter-mile or so beyond the tunnel's southern portal the line passed under another S&SJR structure, a bridge taking a lane into Oxted Lime Works on the down side. This bridge has also had to make way for the rather larger one carrying the M25 over the line, the remains of the extensive quarry visible north of the motorway being reached, unsurprisingly, from Chalkpit Lane. The works were rail connected from 1886, the junction with the Down line, at 19m 8ch from London Bridge, being controlled by the small 'Oxted Lime Sidings' signal box on the Up side. This closed in March 1933 though it would seem rail-borne traffic did not cease until 1939. However, the connection lasted until 1969, the sidings being lifted two years later. The quarry connection also marks a steepening of the downward gradient to 1 in 100.

At 20 miles and 25 chains from London Bridge the line reaches Oxted, the most important intermediate station on the route. It stands on a short stretch of 1 in 300 and opened originally as Oxted & Limpsfield, the latter village being a mile away to the east. As mentioned earlier, the station is also some way from Oxted itself, which is nowadays known as Old Oxted to distinguish it from this newer and more substantial community.

On 26 August 1950 'I3' No 32076 is at Culver junction with an Oxted to Brighton service running via East Grinstead. This was the last year of operation for this engine as it was withdrawn at the end of December. *S C Nash/Stephenson Locomotive Society.*

Typical SER timber buildings were erected on the Up side with an arc-roofed shelter on the Down platform, a subway – also for general public use – providing connection between the two sides of the station. The signal box, at the country end of the Down platform, was moved further south in 1889 on lengthening of the platform for provision of a bay. This was for use of connecting trains destined for Tunbridge Wells via Edenbridge, that line having opened in October the previous year. The bay is not now, nor indeed ever was, accessible from the Up line, terminating trains arriving at the Up platform and shunting across. From quite early days such trains were, in the main, worked on the 'pull/push' principle to simplify matters. The bay line is not electrified, neither is that in the up bay, the latter simply identified nowadays as 'Long Dock'.

The Oxted & Limpsfield Gas Company opened their works on the east side of the station in 1885 – the gasholder is still there – and a chute was provided in 1896 to send coal directly into the premises from a siding put in four years earlier alongside the bay line.

The goods yard, on the up side with its connections at the south end, at first consisted of only two sidings in addition to a loading bank alongside the short up bay, with a further siding from the head shunt into a large sandpit. The yard capacity was increased as the community grew, gradually taking up most of the sandpit until at Grouping eight sidings were available as well as a goods shed, warehouse, end loading dock and a 6-ton crane. The yard was the last on the line to close, in January 1969, all but one of the sidings, then used for stock storage, eventually being lifted. The gasworks siding lasted until 1986

though it had not been used for its original purpose for years.

As with other stations on the line, both platforms were lengthened in 1963, at the London end in Oxted's case, to accommodate the new diesel-electric trains which, in rush hours, could be nine coaches long (three three-car DEMU sets). A further lengthening to twelve coaches was completed in 2010.

The timber station building, which had rotted very badly under an application of render applied shortly after nationalisation, was demolished at the beginning of 1987 and a new brick-built structure in the same 'chalet' style as at Sanderstead brought into use in September. In the interim the up bay housed a BR-type 2EPB unit which acted as a mobile, albeit at the time 'static', waiting room. The building underwent a full refurbishment in 2010.

The signal box at Oxted closed in July 1987 upon opening of a new brick-built panel box situated next to the down bay at its junction with the down line. This has control of the lines to both East Grinstead and Uckfield, from south of Riddlesdown in the down direction and of Woldingham viaduct in the up.

Eight chains south of Oxted the line crosses another CO&EGR girder-built structure, the 130-yard long Limpsfield viaduct spanning the main A25 road as it plunges into and out of a steep-sided valley, and twelve chains further on enters Limpsfield tunnel. This is the last of the three built by the S&SJR and is 565 yards long, driven through an outcrop of Gault clay.

The downward gradient has already resumed its steeper fall, now at 1 in 132/100, and at 21 miles and 20 chains the line reaches Hurst Green station. This provides a salutary lesson in unfortunate forward planning. Originally a 'halt' south of the road bridge carrying Greenhurst Road over the line, it opened with a number of others in 1907 in an effort to capture new business as property development occurred in the vicinity. For this purpose it was only moderately successful and consequently closed in June 1961 upon opening of the existing station, which is immediately north of the road bridge. This replacement stopping place although constructed by British Railways was still very much in the SR style; brick buildings with rendered, green-painted panels in the walls, wide, pre-cast concrete platforms, a pre-fabricated concrete footbridge and SR hexagonal lampshades were obvious pointers to its origins. The platforms are twelve coaches long because BR fully intended to divide and join trains here, ample staff quarters also provided for the shunters and train crews. Unfortunately the scheme never came to fruition and was never likely to once the Beeching closures began to bite. Oxted though remains the 'junction' station for East Grinstead and Uckfield line trains which part company fifteen chains further south, at Hurst Green Junction, the line to Uckfield bearing away south-eastwards while that to East Grinstead now assumes a more southerly direction to enter the valley of the River Eden. This lies on Wealden clay, once an important material in brickmaking. The signal box at the junction was demolished shortly after closure in July 1987.

The 1 in 100 gradient resumes until the double-track spur to the SER route between Redhill and Tonbridge left the East Grinstead line on the Down side at Crowhurst Junction North, 23m 35ch from London Bridge. From this point on we are in pure ex-LBSCR territory. A station was proposed here at opening and on several subsequent occasions before the end of the 19th century. Its purpose though could only have been for interchange as road access is non-existent to this day and the community widely scattered. The situation was not helped as neither the SER nor the Brighton were willing to invest in a station that would likely create very little originating use, nor was either willing to see the other benefit from interchange business. The spur and its North and South signal boxes saw their last train in October 1965.

Having passed over two separate streams of the Eden and under the Redhill-Tonbridge line, our route has to surmount a short uphill length at 1 in 100/200 before it dips down again at 1 in 152 to pass the site of 'Lingfield Intermediate' box (24m 42ch). This also conveniently controlled access to the sidings of the Lingfield Brick & Tile Works. It was downgraded to a ground frame in August 1958, local access being released by Lingfield station box: the connection was in use until around 1970.

Lingfield stands 26 miles 23 chains from London Bridge and marks the end of the falling gradient from Oxted. The station opened with the line in 1884 but was extensively rebuilt ten years later following the increase in traffic to the adjacent racecourse established in 1890. This work included widening the Down platform and was to form an island, though the rails laid on its Down side could be accessed only from the Down end when first brought into use in May 1894. A connection at the London end to complete the loop had to wait until November. At the same time a berthing siding was laid off the

loop's up end and another added alongside that. The points at the south end were worked by a ground frame which only came into use for race day traffic.

On the Up side, the platform was lengthened to provide an up bay for use on race days; a footbridge added at the south end of the platforms facilitated movement of race-goers to a covered way that led directly to the course. This lasted *in situ* until 1982, though it had been out of use for some time before being sold to the Bluebell Railway and re-erected at Sheffield Park.

The station buildings and goods yard were on the up side of the line, the former in very grand and typical Brighton architectural style with the two-storey stationmaster's house incorporated in the structure. It is now a listed building. The goods yard contained a dock road and three long, well spaced sidings with a connection at the London end. Along with the up bay, it closed in 1968 though banana traffic to the Geest facility north of the station continued until transferred to road transport three years later. All sidings were lifted in 1974 as was the Down loop.

Down trains leaving Lingfield are faced with 1½ miles at 1 in 70 almost off the platform end as the line climbs out of the Eden valley to surmount the sandy ridge of the Tunbridge Wells Beds on which East Grinstead stands. The gradient eases to 1 in 210 through the rather remote Dormans station (27m 62ch) which, though the line approaches on embankment, lies in a cutting. The station building, another superb Brighton structure of the period, stands at road level on the east side of the cutting. A lengthy staircase, once roofed, leads directly out of the booking hall to a footbridge to the platforms. There were two sidings here but neither intended for public use. Instead the one on the up side served the needs of the adjacent House of St Barnabas, built in the early years of the 20th century as a home for retired clergymen. The other formed a refuge on the Down side approaches. There were otherwise no goods facilities.

On leaving Dormans the line immediately resumes its 1 in 70 climb, passing the site of a siding on the up side that served the Dormans Park Estate, the probable reason for the fine station building. Here the cutting gives way to embankment as the track approaches and levels out to cross Cooks Pond viaduct, three quarters of a mile from Dormans. This functional though impressive CO&EGR structure, of five 125'-long girder spans, carries the rails 65' above the water. The lake is not natural but made by damming a stream crossing the Dormans Park Estate en route to the Eden. The lake also had to be drained to permit construction of the bridge pier foundations.

The climb resumes immediately at 1 in 67/70 until reaching the site of St Margaret's Junction (29m 41ch) where the line once divided. Heading straight on, as trains do today, takes the route over easier gradients into what once were the low-level platforms at East Grinstead, 30 miles 5 chains from London Bridge. Forking to the right, as Tunbridge Wells-bound trains used to do, the line continued to climb at 1 in 70, latterly on a tightly-curved double track spur, to make a trailing junction with the route from Three Bridges immediately to the west of the station's upper level, making a journey 12 chains longer than to the low level.

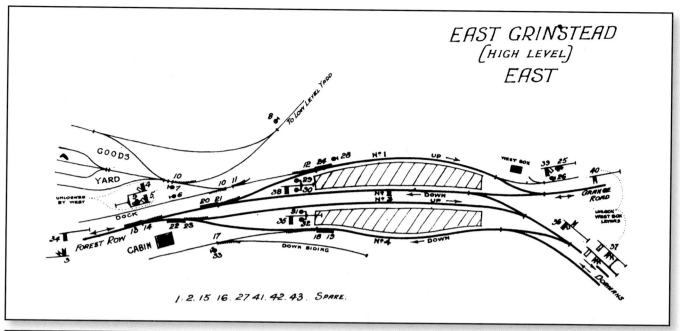

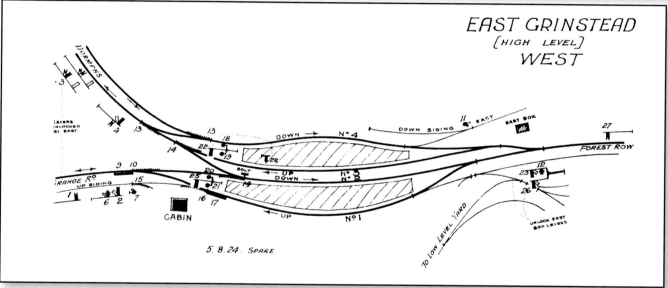

A recent find was a number of signal box diagrams which fortunately included the various boxes at East Grinstead. Those shown are for the High Level station, respectively 'west' and 'east' and which were renamed 'A' and 'B' from 15 September 1958. Both ceased to control trains from 2 January 1967.

This is the third site for the station serving the town. The first opened in 1855 a little to the east and on the site of what became part of the goods yard, and the second with the line to Groombridge in 1866, further east still and adjacent to London Road.

The upper level of this third station, placed here because the Brighton was not prepared to pay the asking price for the conveniently-placed timber yard also just to the east, consisted of two island platforms. These were of timber where they spanned the tracks below, with wooden platform buildings: the four tracks from the north were Down, Up, Down, Up. The lower platforms and main station building stood to the south of the bridge carrying the upper level. Staircases east and west

of the lower lines connected the two levels though after provision of a footbridge between the lower platforms in 1891 the western staircase was closed. The very substantial two-storey brick building, plentifully hung with tiles – Sheffield Park on a larger scale! – stood on the Down side of the line and contained accommodation for the stationmaster as well as a large and ornate refreshment room. It was demolished in 1970, to be replaced by a nondescript 'CLASP' building which opened in 1972. That too has now gone, a much improved and more substantial and suitable structure coming into use in December 2012, though official opening wasn't until the turn of the year, in part in celebration of the Bluebell Railway reaching the town.

Apart from the St Margaret's loop, a single east to south spur running between the sidings of the lower goods yard also joined the two levels. This was used purely for shunting and empty stock movements and, by completing a triangle, the occasional turning of locomotives.

The low level station was rarely used after final closure of the line to Lewes in 1958. This changed when the high level lines closed with the abandonment of the Three Bridges-Ashurst Junction route in January 1967 and subsequent demolition of the upper level. All trains then terminated at and departed from the lower level down platform though the Up one was later reinstated for use at busy times. Electrification in 1987 saw the crossovers between Up and Down lines north of the station taken out and a short stretch of single track interposed to save on point work.

The goods yard closed in April 1967 though a number of sidings remained in place for a further twenty years to hold empty stock. A stub of the former line to Lewes towards Imberhorne viaduct still serves this purpose.

The site for the Bluebell Railway's platform, to the south and on the down side of the BR station, was cleared in May 2008. Preparation for tracklaying commenced in November and track had reached the landfill site in Hill Place cutting, south of Imberhorne viaduct, by June 2010. Its initial purpose was to enable trains of waste to be worked away from the cutting to a disposal site at Calvert, Buckinghamshire. The first

Diagrams for the north and south boxes at the low level station, respectively. 'South' was renamed 'C' on the same date as described before it was again closed at the same time as the 'A' and 'B'. 'North' however had been closed some years before and ceased operation in October 1928.

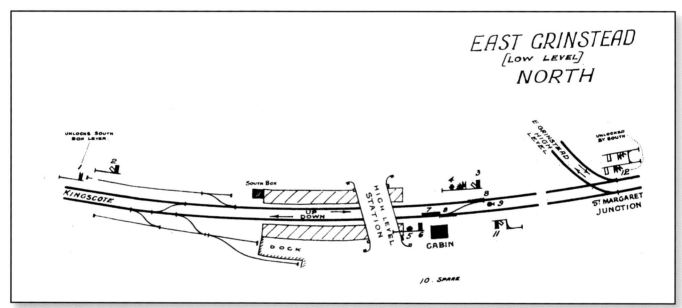

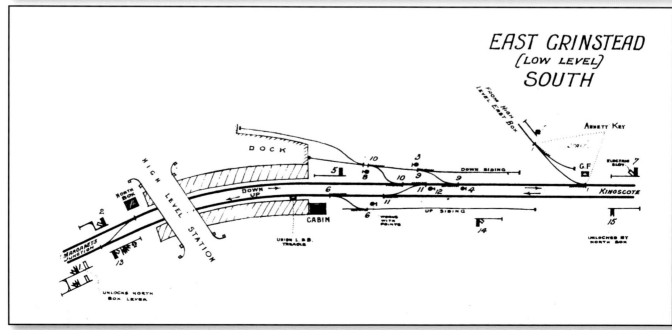

of these ran on 6 July. The first 'through' Bluebell service, behind the inimitable 'Terrier', No 55, *Stepney*, departed East Grinstead at 9.45 am on 23 March 2013. It is a nice touch, a neat piece of history perhaps, that the road past the station and leading to Sainsbury's store and the car park near the Bluebell terminus should also be named Firbank Way.

Early responsibility for signalling the line north of Crowhurst Junction was shared by both the Brighton and South Eastern companies, signal boxes being of individual company design. Most were of wood on brick or stone bases though Oxted and Crowhurst North boxes were timber-built throughout. Some of the Brighton's massive tapered timber signal posts lasted into the late-1950s though by then their distinctive wooden signal arms had mostly given way to SR pressed steel upper quadrants. The last complete ex-LBSCR signal on BR survived until May 1971, at Hurst Green Junction. The section between South Croydon and Riddlesdown viaduct (Down direction) and Woldingham viaduct (Up) was converted to power signalling controlled from the Three Bridges centre in 1985. The remainder, as already noted, is now the responsibility of Oxted.

A steady increase in passenger traffic resulted in twenty-five trains being scheduled each way between South Croydon and Oxted on weekdays by 1914, with Tunbridge Wells as the primary destination. Three other services emanated from or went to London Bridge via Woodside though these were withdrawn in 1915. From that time the service pattern underwent continuing evolution with many adjustments too numerous to note here. By 1939 about half the thirty-six trains through Oxted ran to East Grinstead, most continuing onward either to Brighton via Lewes or to Tunbridge Wells West via Forest Row. The remainder took the direct route to Tunbridge Wells via Edenbridge Town, where most terminated, though again a proportion made for the coast at Brighton or Eastbourne.

Alone among services in the Southern's commuter belt, no attempt was made to introduce a regular interval pattern, which had to wait until 1955 and a completely recast timetable. London Bridge retained only its rush-hour trains, the off-peak service being concentrated at Victoria leaving at eight minutes past each hour. This ran to Tunbridge Wells West via East Grinstead and Forest Row in 74 minutes, making a connection at Oxted into trains taking the more direct route via Edenbridge Town in an overall time nineteen minutes less. But even this pattern was disrupted, the 11.08 am for example continuing to run as a through service to Brighton and Eastbourne, a Tunbridge Wells West via East Grinstead portion being detached at East Croydon. It was a short-lived change as a year later it reverted to pattern following the introduction of regular interval working on the Uckfield and Heathfield lines. The few remaining trains between Victoria and the South Coast via Oxted continued to run interspersed within the regular hourly pattern.

'C2X' No 32526 at Oxted with two three-coach sets: one new BR Mk 1 stock and the other Bulleid vehicles. The service is facing south towards Hurst Green Junction and from the head code is an Oxted to Brighton train running via the East Grinstead Low Level (and therefore the Bluebell line) and Lewes.
N E Stead

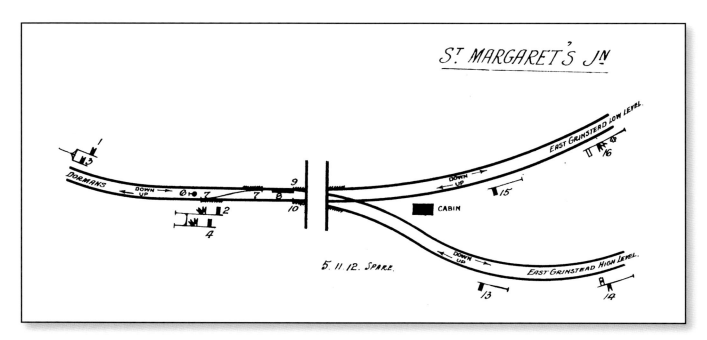

Diagram for St Margaret's Junction north of East Grinstead.

Dieselisation saw the pattern continue but at electrification the East Grinstead service became half-hourly with trains starting and terminating at Victoria and London Bridge alternately, though only the former features now except in weekday rush hours. The Uckfield line remains diesel-operated in 2019, all subsequent proposals for electrification failing to make an economic case. Classes 170 and 171 'Turbostar' units took over from the 'Thumpers' in 2005, which seems to have quashed any pro-electrification arguments for the foreseeable future. This is even more surprising given that the hourly Uckfield line trains now provide a 'fast' service right through to/from the Capital – and that is over 21½ miles of electrified track north of Hurst Green! – calling intermediately only at East Croydon between Oxted and London Bridge. The hourly Oxted connection is, however, retained on Sundays.

Busy times at Oxted on 13 May 1948 with three trains all facing south. Nearest the camera in the yard is 'Q' No 540, this displays an Oxted to Tunbridge Wells West via East Grinstead HL route disc. Next is 'I3' No 32075, again with an Oxted to Brighton via the Bluebell line code, and finally a 'D1' No 2253 on an unreported passenger working. *E R Wethersett*

Most freight traffic was handled from/to Norwood Yard, generally with Norwood engines and crews, up to four trains being required each way latterly though not all called at all stations. The 10.18 am Up from East Grinstead for example served Lingfield, Lingfield Brick Siding, if required, and Selsdon while the 5.05 am down called only at Selsdon before terminating at Oxted.

In BR days the bulk of steam-worked passenger traffic over the CO&EGR line involved engines – mainly Fairburn and, later, BR 'Standard' class 4 tanks – and crews from Tunbridge Wells West and Stewarts Lane sheds with Brighton, Bricklayers Arms and Three Bridges also claiming a share.* (Through services to the coast, particularly via Uckfield, were more often in the charge of Maunsell 'Moguls'.) All though was swept away by closures and dieselisation, the first of the class '3D' three-car 'Thumper' units entering service in June 1962, with steam working vanishing by the end of the year. Surplus two- and three-car 'Hampshire' units were drafted in from late-1965 and even 'Hastings' six-car sets appeared from time to time. All the diesels were maintained at St Leonards, which required much light running, especially after the Uckfield-Lewes connection was severed in 1969.

*I once had an unauthorised footplate ride on a BR 'Std 4MT' between South Croydon and Oxted with a Norwood crew. This had come about as the fireman was a friend and the driver turned a blind eye. I never found out if this was a regular Norwood duty or simply a 'one-off'. Many Norwood men would have signed for the road of course.

A number of rush-hour trains continued to be locomotive-hauled by the Southern Region's very capable class '33' diesel-electrics. One carriage rake consisted of former 2BIL unit No 2006 which, stripped of motors and shoe gear, sandwiched five ex-4SUB augmentation trailers, one of which had had 1st class reinstated. This unit, which came into service in 1963, was numbered 900 but later, classified as a '7TC', it became 701. Despite having driving cabs at both ends there was never any suggestion of using the unit in push/pull mode. It was withdrawn in 1969, the trailers being reused but the old BIL vehicles going for scrap.

After some spasmodic testing and an 'official opening', the full electrified service between London and East Grinstead was introduced on 5 October 1987 using 4-CIG and 4-VEP sets with 2-EPB strengtheners at the peaks. The 4-VEPs came to dominate, selected sets being fitted with bars across the droplights in case of chalk falls in the unlined sections of Oxted tunnel. Nowadays the regular half-hourly off-peak service is worked by class '377' stock. Only Clapham Junction is served between Victoria and East Croydon but then all stations from Sanderstead in an overall time of fifty-five minutes down and fifty-eight minutes up. Uckfield trains to/from London Bridge run fast to Oxted with the one intermediate call at East Croydon, and then all stations onward in seventy-three minutes down, seventy-eight minutes up. As they travel beyond the London Suburban area all trains provide first class accommodation.

An unreported 'C2X', this time on a freight turn arriving at Oxted from the south, likely from Tunbridge Wells. *Derek Clayton*

The north end of Oxted where 'C2X' No 1248 is seen taking water. In the background another passenger train is approaching but with an unidentified headcode. Note the water column in its striped colouring, a throwback to wartime blackout restrictions, whilst the man on the right has to wait to cross the line; not only does he have the approaching train to contend with but the 'C2X' is also obstructing the board crossing. *Derek Clayton*

This level of service makes the CO&EGR as busy now as at any time since WW2 and, indeed, for some time before it despite the loss of 'through' workings to the coast. Whether or not reinstatement of the Uckfield-Lewes line, much in the public eye at the time of writing, goes ahead, surely the ultimate anachronism in this otherwise fully electrified area is retention of diesel working over those bare 24¾ route miles to the southern Sussex terminus.

Bibliography:

'Croydon (Woodside) to East Grinstead',
    Vic Mitchell & Keith Smith, Middleton Press, 1995.

'Branch Lines to East Grinstead',
    Vic Mitchell & Keith Smith, Middleton Press,
    1984 (5th reprint 2005).

'The London, Brighton & South Coast Railway',
    C Hamilton Ellis, Ian Allan Ltd., 1960.

'History of the Southern Railway', C F Dendy Marshall,
    revised by R W Kidner, Ian Allan Ltd., 1963 (1982 Reprint).

'The Croydon, Oxted & East Grinstead Railway', David Gould,
    The Oakwood Press, 2003.

'Sussex Railways Remembered', Leslie Oppitz,
    Countryside Books, 1987.

'Croydon's Railways', M W G Skinner,
    Kingfisher Railway Productions, 1985.

'Railways of the Southern Region', Geoffrey Body,
    Patrick Stephens Ltd., 1984 (1989 reprint).

'Southern Electric Album', Alan Williams, Ian Allan Ltd., 1977.

'British Railway Tunnels', Alan Blower, Ian Allan Ltd., 1964.

'Atlas of the Southern Railway',
    Richard Hardman & Gerry Nichols,
    Ian Allan Publishing Ltd., 2016.

'British Rail Mainline Gradient Profiles',
    Ian Allan in collaboration with Tothill Press.

'Railway Track Diagrams' No 5, England South and London
    Underground, Quail Map Company, 2nd edition 2002.

Ordnance Survey Landranger map No 187, (Dorking &
    Reigate), Crown copyright, 2003.

A-Z Street Atlas, Croydon/Purley/Sutton/ Mitcham,
    Geographers A-Z map Co. Ltd., Sevenoaks, 2009.

Southern train times No 18, East Grinstead and Oxted to
    Croydon and London, 21 May 2017 to 19 May 2018.

Some websites have been studied, mainly for confirmatory information, that of the Southern E-Group being particularly helpful in that respect. Google maps have provided a view of stations I have not been able to visit recently. Inevitably the timetables of Southern Rail were scanned for accurate travel information at the time of writing.

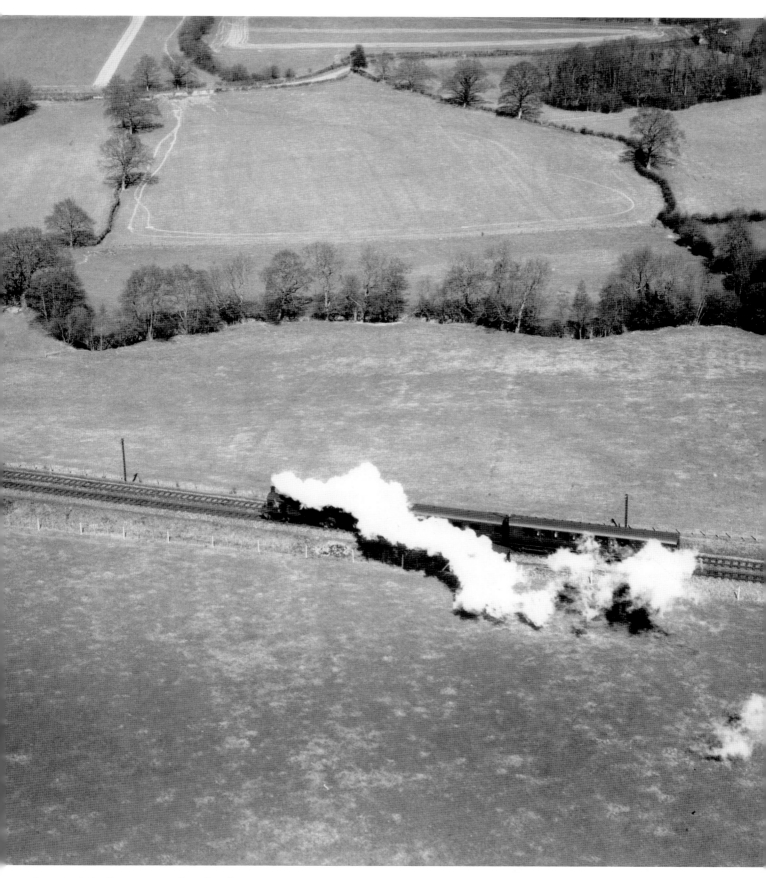

Steam in the landscape – near Ashurst (Kent).

Pulverised Fuel Part 1
No A629

On 29 December 1929 a brand new member of the 'U' class, 2-6-0 No A629, left Ashford works having been fitted for experimental purposes with a German 'AEG'* designed burner and turbine intended to burn pulverised fuel – coal dust. Over the following 34 months No A629 ran just 3,497 miles in its experimental guise (equivalent to little more than an average of 100 miles per month – less than 25 miles per week), punctuated it seems by long periods stored out of use, only relieved by its occasional forays on to the running lines, during which time it seemed to leave behind a trail of dense clouds of dusty smoke, which were often blamed for lineside fires. (No doubt there was some truth in this with the solicitors acting for the Southern Railway likely kept busy dealing with rather more compensation claims than usual. A similar picture arose in the last months of steam in 1967, when, with speed restrictions lifted and a few drivers prepared to 'have a last fling', there resulted in rather more claims for compensation from another generation of farmers who might just have happened to build a hayrick a bit closer to the railway than was usual… . It was not just the operators nor a publicity department who would heave a sign of relief when 10 July 1967 came… .)

The intention of the conversion of No A629 was clearly an attempt to achieve some saving in coal costs, not withstanding the already known policy of the SR towards future electrification.

Before delving further into the story of No A629, it is necessary to set the scene as regards the use of this type of fuel and which is best known in the work carried out by J G Robinson on the Great Central Railway almost a decade before. Robinson had been attracted by the possibility of using a lower grade of coal, which in its pulverised form might be mixed with oil to form a colloidal fuel. A total of five of his various 2-8-0 engines were converted for experimental purposes, one (No 966) being modified with a special firebox especially designed for the fuel being tried. An experimental oil and pulverised fuel plant was installed at Gorton and it is believed came into use around January 1920. The various experiments appear to have been successful

with a technical observer reporting that an engine so fitted (we are not told if this was No 966 or one of the other four) was observed from the footplate working a 500 ton train between Gorton and Dunfold to schedule and without delaying other similar weight trains following behind. (Reference: https://www.advanced-steam.org/wp-content/uploads/2017/07/Brown-Coal-Dust-Firing-for-Locomotives.pdf)

According to Michael Rutherford in his very useful article in Vol 9 of 'Backtrack' (January 1995, pp33 – 38), other fuel experiments carried out by the GCR around the same time involved using both creosote and pitch as fuel; the pervading aroma from which might only be imagined. Robinson had used

A general view of No A629 taken by H C Casserley at its home shed of Eastbourne on 20 February 1932. This was probably before the 'explosion' referred to later in the text and the engine's subsequent transfer to Ashford. In the photograph it appears out of steam, whilst considering the limited mileage run in this modified form the engine would probably have spent much time like this – literally standing around.

* The initials 'AEG' stand for the 'Allgemeine Elektricitäts-Gesellschaft', i.e. Universal Electricity Company.

pulverising equipment sourced from the USA and whilst the results showed promise, they had been obtained in the main by pulverising an existing high-grade black coal. We are not told if similar experiments took place with a low-grade fuel, or indeed if this was the case, what results were obtained. The whole appears to have been curtailed shortly after the LNER takeover of the GCR with the official announcement that there was nothing to be gained in pulverising a fuel that would burn perfectly well in its raw format.

Elsewhere though it was a different matter and especially in countries where the most readily available fuel was in fact 'brown coal' or 'lignite' as it is sometimes known. This type of fuel was readily available in parts of the USA but so far as this story is concerned we should really mention Germany and Poland. Consequently it was really only logical that a scheme was developed to burn this type of fuel in Eastern Europe. German engineers also played a lead role and with two distinct players, firstly the 'STUG' system based around a consortium of locomotive builders and mine syndicates, and also the AEG system referred to previously.

'Brown coal' from its very consist does not need the amount of crushing to produce dust whereas, as the GCR had found, 'black' coal needed a far heavier pulverising treatment. This could of course have been done on the SR but according to H Holcroft** would have involved a heavy increase in costs.

The internet source referred to earlier also makes mention of the use of this type of fuel in Australia (there is some confusion as to whether this was in Victoria or New South Wales) where although relatively successful, there was excessive noise in the cab caused by the necessary auxiliary equipment. Other countries which at some time or other used or experimented with pulverised fuel included Sweden (this was in 1913 and involved pulverised peat), and later in Hungary, Brazil and Italy. In the latter the experiments were rapidly curtailed owing to fire damage to the pulverising plant – a story that also came close to being repeated on the SR later.

** Locomotive Adventure Vol 2: Running Experiences', pp 77 /78. Pub Ian Allan 1965.

Rear side views of the modified tender fitted to No A629 – note in one of the images the tender coupling is missing. (Was this a deliberate ploy to prevent a harassed shed-foreman from 'borrowing' the engine if short of motive power?) In front stands 'Terrier' No 751 which was seconded to the trials to act as an auxiliary steam supply to the hopper and coal crusher when required. Might No 751 have also acted as an external 'blower' to No A629 on occasions as well?) High up towards the front of the tender are what appear to be clips, perhaps to hold a flap or casing? The purpose of the inspection covers on the rear is not certain but may well have been a means of access to the feed screws. At the rear, the box on the back with the slatted louvers contained the steam driven turbine providing compressed air for the feed screws. *H C Casserley and C L Turner*

When referring to pulverised peat as a fuel in Sweden, it should be stated there is no connection here with the time decades later when Mr Bulleid used the same fuel in his locomotive 'CC1' in Ireland. Peat was indeed used again but not in such a fine form and consequently no pulverising took place – other than of course in the natural breakage of the fuel that occurred in consequence of it being fed by an Archimedean screw from the bunker to the firebox.

Most significantly the same internet report reveals the interesting result that, when tested, the Australian (Victoria state) locomotive showed almost identical boiler and furnace efficacy when comparing the use of pulverised brown coal against hard fired black coal.

Whether the Southern Railway were approached by AEG or made the approach themselves cannot be determined with any certainty. On the basis of the foregoing it would appear more likely it was the SR who made the approach, this conclusion being based on the success the pulverising system had achieved elsewhere, although without available dates for the other episodes described this must for the present remain conjecture.

As converted No A629 was based at Eastbourne, where an unsuspecting public had not, it seems, been informed of what was to come, even if a hundred or so miles away others were better informed. This was in consequence of a short piece that appeared in the *Western Gazette* newspaper, which circulated in Somerset dated 20 September 1929. Under the headline, 'Dust Fuel Experiments on the Southern Railway', the article informed its readers that the Southern Railway was to try, "...a new system for the burning of pulverised fuel in locomotive boilers." Not only clearly a 'quiet news day' but the writer concerned also had no idea that it was the boiler that did just that – boiled water – the actual burning took place in the firebox!

Eastbourne shed was also where the necessary pulverising plant was likewise installed. Again, we know from Holcroft that reports on the working of the engine were passed to the SR Headquarters but other than stating he read them, Holcroft does little to elaborate further. Consequently the best source for information as to operation of the engine is D L Bradley in his work: 'The Locomotive History of the South Eastern & Chatham Railway'. (RCTS 1980.)

From this source approximately a column and a half is devoted to the story of No A629 in its modified form and we learn that the provision of the tender bunker to hold the pulverised fuel restricted the water capacity to 3,300 gallons compared to the usual 3,500 gallons. Fuel capacity was 296cu.ft. There were three screws for delivering the fuel to the firebox (see later description), the two outer ones used for the main feed and a central smaller screw for auxiliary requirements. Each was driven through gears and a separate steam engine mounted on the tender front. As will have been immediately gathered, the locomotive and tender were an 'item' and whilst could obviously be separated if required, there was no interchange for either with any other member of the 'U' class whilst No A629 was running in its modified form. In operation, fuel was forced from the ends of the screws via necessary flexible connections between the loco and tender and thence to the firebox using compressed air.

The compressed air for the main feeds came from a fan operated by a steam turbine on the rear of the tender and from a belt-driven steam engine for the auxiliary feed. This auxiliary feed was intended for lighting-up with the fuel arriving in the firebox from the rear, the main fuel feeds entering from the sides.

Within the firebox, the grate as such had been removed and replaced with firebricks although an ashpan was retained. Another modification was the ability to effectively seal the tender front when refuelling was taking place and so keep the cab and footplate free of dust. How effective this was is not reported nor were general conditions on the footplate.

Initial trials were conducted from Ashford but at the end of January 1930 the engine was moved to Eastbourne, where its performance would be judged against sister engine No A627. For the purpose both engines were also fitted with speedometers.

It is information on these comparative trials and indeed most of the other runs that is lacking, although Bradley comments No 1629 was "...very temperamental and seldom entrusted with important trains". Whether this was indeed mechanical/fuel issues or unfamiliarity by the crew is not stated. In similar vein we are not told if a specific 'test' crew was employed or if an Inspector/Instructor was present. Certainly there must have been some formal instruction given, for this was a totally different machine to operate compared to a coal fired machine, especially in respect of the fireman's duties. Jumping ahead one may even ask if the men were simply being left to 'get on with it'? If so, does this go part way to explain why there were so many issues with performance and lineside fires?

According to A Elsey writing in the 'R.O' in the early 1940s, "No A629 was rarely used on important trains...", but unlike other experiments which were usually kept away from passenger workings, No A629 did once work the prestige 'Southern Belle' and according to Bradley "to time". Over what distance this occurred is not stated. (With no wish to appear deliberately sceptical, could it have been that whoever had authorised/suggested the conversion in the first place also felt the need to ensure No A629 was seen fit to work a passenger service, if for no other reason than to justify both the experiment and perhaps even its continuation? A similar situation occurred some years later with No 2039, the 'Atlantic' equipped with sleeve valves, when it was felt necessary to 'prove' the venture. On the latter occasion, however, the result was not so successful and No 2039 failed. But if 'justification' was indeed the reason for No A629 appearing in public, why was it then not repeated?)

We know No A629 also visited Eastleigh in October 1930 ostensibly to familiarise the staff there which in itself immediately asks the question 'why'? Were more conversions planned, or could it have been simply for 'engineering interest'?

No changes appear to have been made at Eastleigh then or subsequently and what modifications that were made were undertaken at Brighton over a four-month period from March to July 1931. These were intended to address the issue of unburnt fuel being ejected through the chimney and no doubt the cause of the lineside fires referred to.

Taken from the *Southern Railway Magazine* this is the only known view of the engine actually working a train and a fair load at that consisting of ten vehicles and at least one Pullman car. We are not informed what working this might have been although speculation has to be it was the 'Southern Belle' turn.

According to one source, Bradley, the general behaviour of the engine was not successful and he quotes, "…No A629's progress through the Sussex countryside was marked by dense clouds of dirty smoke, lineside fires and the sound of fire engines." But this is contradicted by Elsey, who in what was a very short piece covering three separate SR locomotive experiments, Nos 1816, 1629 and 1850 (No A629 had been renumbered as 1629 by the time of the article), "As so often occurs, the apparatus was successful, the high maintenance costs more than counteracted the saving in fuel costs".

Bradley also contradicts himself slightly when he states that the one success of the trials was the special bunker at Eastbourne to contain the pulverised fuel and prevent spillage. (It is believed there was no coal crusher provided at the depot so where was the fuel actually pulverised and similarly how was it delivered?) But he then goes on to say that on one occasion this bunker "…displayed distinct signs of being about to explode" and had to be emptied into waiting wagons. The final consequence was something that might have been part of a contemporary Charlie Chaplin or similar film had it not had a serious result, in that with as much fuel as possible removed from the bunker, the blowers (?) were turned on and the residue fuel immediately ignited with a thunderous crash resulting in a dense cloud of black smoke being deposited over much of Eastbourne. One suspects both the station master and shed foreman made themselves scarce rather quickly. Somewhat surprisingly, both this episode and indeed the earlier arrival of the engine at Eastbourne, whilst reported in the press elsewhere, appear not to have been noted in the local newspapers.

After this 'event' came the transfer of the engine back to Ashford for further modification and again according to Bradley, working thereafter from that shed, but without further elaboration. We are also not told what bunkering facilities were provided at Ashford. Having realistically failed to show any real advantage No A629 was recalled to Ashford works in October 1932, where it was restored to conventional condition and returned to service at the end of the same year. The component parts removed were later cut up for scrap in the wartime drive for metal around mid-1942 although this ten-year delay could also suggest the future idea of further trials.

Holcroft adds a comment that the trials were likely not a success as the firebox of No A629 was not ideal and the hard coal used needed a far greater degree of pulverising – echoing the same comments as the GCR. On the SR this had not been done and was, he states, the cause of the sparks being emitted. Similar sentiment was apparently made by Messrs AEG.

Holcroft continued, "…the amount of fine white dust ejected from chimney in the form of powder made it unsuitable for passenger use unless trains were air-conditioned, but this drawback does not apply to goods services. In the case of coal, all the impurities which normally form clinker and ash are pulverised along with the combustible and so form droplets of molten slag which passes through the boiler tubes." Perhaps this was also the first time mention of air-conditioned coaches is made by an SR engineer. One may wonder then about the experience of the passengers on the 'Southern Belle' with No A629 at its head?

A fortunate find was at the National Railway Museum where within the papers of the late J G Click there survives a set of instructions for the preparation and servicing of the engine in its experimental guise.

A tantalising view of No A629 somewhere other than Eastbourne. (From the turntable might this even be outside London Bridge [or Victoria]?) If so, then we have proof of one of the locations worked to, but again it throws up more questions, service train or trial? We are also treated to a view of the turbine in operation on the rear of the tender whilst the head code will be noted as being the same as that seen in the previous 'train' view. *Stephenson Locomotive Society*

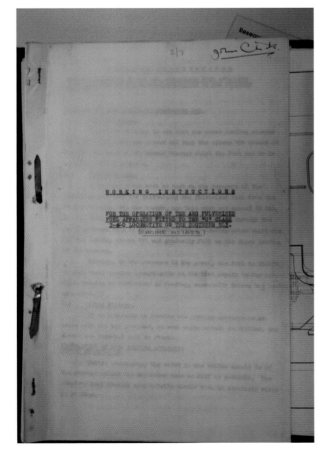

Working Instructions for the operation of the AEG pulverised fuel apparatus fitted to 'U' Class 2-6-0 locomotive No A629 of the Southern Railway.

1. Charging the bunker with compressed air.

a) Before filling, care must be taken to see that the screw sealing sleeves 'V' are closed and the sieves 'S' placed at the filling holes of the bunker, through which fuel has to be charged, are in position.

b) During filling, a constant watch must be kept on the pressure of the compressed air used for discharging the pulverised fuel from the container wagon into the bunker, and this must not exceed 21lbs. psi. The fuel is otherwise liable to feed through the gap (although this is very small) between the feeding screw shaft and the sealing sleeve 'V' and gradually fill up the pipes leading to the burners. Further, if the pressure is too great, the fuel is liable to pack tight causing irregularities in the fuel supply to the screws which results in difficulty in feeding, especially during the heating-up period.

c) After filling, it is advisable to revolve the feed screws once or twice with the key provided, as even under normal conditions, the screws are somewhat hard to rotate.

2. Preparation of fuel for feeding apparatus before starting up.

Before commencing, the water in the boiler should be at the correct height and the water tank as full as possible. The complete fuel feeding gear details should then be carefully oiled as follows:

a) Auxiliary steam engine splash lubrication. Before putting into operation for the first time, it is advisable to oil the bearings of all moving parts by means of an oil syringe. These are easily accessible by removing the cover plates on the crank case. Once the crank case covers have been replaced, cock 'F' on the oil separator is closed and the water level cock 'E' is opened. Cap 'B' is removed and water is poured into the air vent pipe revealed until water is seen emerging from cock 'E'. Cock 'E' is then closed and good machine oil, or preferably mineral oil, is poured into the air vent pipe until water emerges from oil level pipe 'D'. To be able to see the water emerging cap 'C' has to be removed. After the correct oil level has been attained, (which is shown by the water emerging) cups 'B' and 'C' are to be replaced. It is especially important to note that cap 'C' is only to be removed for filling water or oil through the air vent pipe, and is to be immediately replaced after filling, otherwise coal dust and dirt is liable to enter the crank case and cause trouble with the bearings. Fresh oil does not require to be added before each journey, as the crank case contains sufficient for several journeys, unless of course the engine is drained after each trip.

b) Pressure oiling apparatus. The chamber with five feeds is to be filled with superheater oil (cylinder oil) and the chamber with four feeds is to be filled with good machine oil. When filling for the first time, the end of the longest oil feed pipe is to be unscrewed and the crank of the pump actuated until oil is effectively fed to the various points. The end is then to be reconnected.

c) Myrel lubrication. The two Myrel lubricators on the bearing covers of the auxiliary engine are to be filled at intervals with warm roller-bearing grease, by means of a syringe. The same applies to the three hind end bearings for the screws. The stuffing boxes of the mixing chambers do not need to be oiled, as the packing is of a type that does not require oiling. The lubricators embodied on the stuffing boxes which are closed with cap nuts are only provided for cases of necessity.

d) Other lubrication. The parts of the governor requiring it can be oiled by means of an oiling syringe. It is important however that the cap at the top end of the spindle guide of the governor should be removed and oil applied to the spindle. The bearing of the intermediate gear wheel on the steam engine is lubricated by means of the Stauffer lubricator placed there, which must be filled before starting up. The driving shaft of the governor is to be lubricated before starting up. The same applies to the water pump piston rod guide, as well as the eccentric for the pump drive.

3. Heating up the locomotive.

The heating period should be about 1½ hours. If required, this period may be considerably lessened, but care must be taken to obviate an unequal heating up of the boiler.

Diagram of the installation. The bunker for the pulverised fuel may be seen as being a form of hopper with the fuel falling to the bottom and then blown by compressed air to the feed screws. Note also the 'tender cab' arrangement.

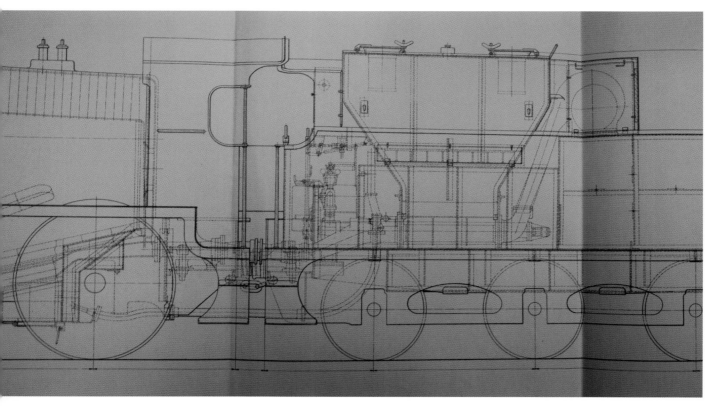

a) Artificial blast. A good blast from the chimney is essential. A portable blower which can be hung inside the chimney is to be used, through which a large volume of compressed air is to be directed until an appreciable blast action is felt in the firebox.

b) Heating up with auxiliary steam. Auxiliary steam at a pressure of 60 to 80lbs psi. is necessary for operating the feeding apparatus and is supplied through valve 'H'. During heating up, this valve is opened, whereas the valve to the boiler 'J' is to be closed. The two-way cock 'A' is to be set so that the steam is exhausted direct to atmosphere. This is to prevent the water condensation present in the pipes entering the steam engine cylinder. When steam only appears at the exhaust, the two-way cock is to be set in the 'Working' direction and the crank rotated by means of the crank handle. The revolutions of the engine are to be regulated to approximately 250rpm by turning the spring case fitted to the governor.

c) Lighting up. It is especially important that the right-hand tender valve be opened before lighting the fire. This valve must never be closed during the time the feeding apparatus is working. After the cooling water is circulating satisfactorily (which can be tested by opening the cock 'K' and seeing the water omitted) a piece of oily waste is thrown into the ashpan as close as possible to the pilot burner. The small blower is next set in operation by drawing out the hand-lever on the right hand side of the engine. As soon as the action of the air is noted on the burning waste, the small feed screw is engaged. If the fuel lights and burns well in the ashpan, the turbine blower 'T' is set in operation at a pressure of 3kg/cm2 (42.6lbs psi) and one of the large screws engaged. Once the large burner is operating, the small screw and pilot burner should be cut out. At 230rpm of the auxiliary engine and with a satisfactory blast the pulverised fuel should burn in a very short time with clear exhaust gases. The small blower should not be cut out too late, as otherwise it is liable to cool the brick arch and brick lining.

d) Heating up with own steam. When the boiler pressure has risen to from 70 to 85 psi, the large screw and turbo fan should be disengaged and the pilot burner once more put into operation. The change-over from auxiliary to own steam is done by opening the steam valve 'J' on the boiler and closing the shut-off valve 'H' on the tender. One large screw is usually quite sufficient for bringing the pressure up to blowing off. If the boiler pressure is sufficiently high, the large screw and blower can be disengaged, as the pilot burner will be quite sufficient until time to start.

e) Checking to see if all is in order. After the apparatus is working with the engine's own steam, the fireman should make certain that both screws are functioning correctly. This he can do by alternately engaging and disengaging both screws. The amount of fuel in the bunker can be checked through the filling hole.

f) Leaving the shed. The pilot burner will usually be found quite sufficient for the journey from the shed to where the train is standing. If the fire burns lightly the steam blower should remain only slightly open and the front ashpan door slightly open.

4. During the trip.

a) Starting. Shortly before starting, the steam blower should be opened fully, also the ashpan door in the direction of travel. The large turbine blower at a stop valve pressure of 40/55psi and one large screw at about 360rpm are put in operation, while the small screw and blower are disengaged. If the blowing off pressure has not been reached before starting, the second large screw is engaged. The lower can be throttled down during the journey. The increase in the revolutions of the auxiliary engine by means of the governor to the maximum of 400-500rpm proportionally increases the amount of fuel fed forward. The quantity of primary air must be increased accordingly to the maximum possible with turbine stop valve pressure of 126lbs psi. At this high output the front ashpan door must be fully open.

b) Smoking. Smoking from the chimney can be obviated by careful handling of the fuel feeding gear, i.e. by regulating the rpm of the steam engine and turbine on one hand, and by the correct opening of the ashpan door on the other. The amount of fuel supplied to the firebox should be in accordance with the amount of steam required at the time. The controlling factors are the strength of blast, the primary air and the quality of the fuel. An experienced fireman will continually watch the chimney from which smoke will be emitted if the screws are feeding too much fuel forward. This is usually the cause of smoke being emitted and can be remedied by reducing the rpm of the auxiliary engine. The fire hole door remains closed during the trip to obviate sudden temperature changes in the firebox, which caused the tubes to leak and adversely effect the brick arch and lining. A good pulverised fuel fire can generally be recognised by clear exhaust gases, increased superheat temperature and mounting steam pressure.

c) The fire when ascending and descending. For long inclines, a strong fire is to be arranged and the boiler filled above the middle of the water gauge glass. On long down grades, it is to be recommended that if water is sufficiently high in the boiler, and the pressure correct, the large feeding screws and the turbine be cut out. The pilot burner and blower are then to be brought into operation.

d) Auxiliary blower. If a large burner is operating shortly before the engine stops, the auxiliary blower is to be turned on so as to obviate the possibility of smoke. etc., being emitted from the firedoor due to the lessening of the suction action from the smokebox when the regulator has been closed.

5. After the trip.

When the locomotive has been brought back to the shed, the auxiliary engine and the pump are to be kept in operation for a short time during the period the locomotive is being examined. This is to protect the burners from the surrounding hot brickwork. If there is any danger of frost, the pipes in which water may condense are to be emptied. This also applies to the auxiliary steam engine, the crank-case of which has been filled with water and which gradually acquires more in operation. The emptying of the water in the steam engine can be done by means of drain cock 'F' which allows the water and oil mixture to escape. Naturally fresh water and oil must be supplied to the crank case before the engine again operates.

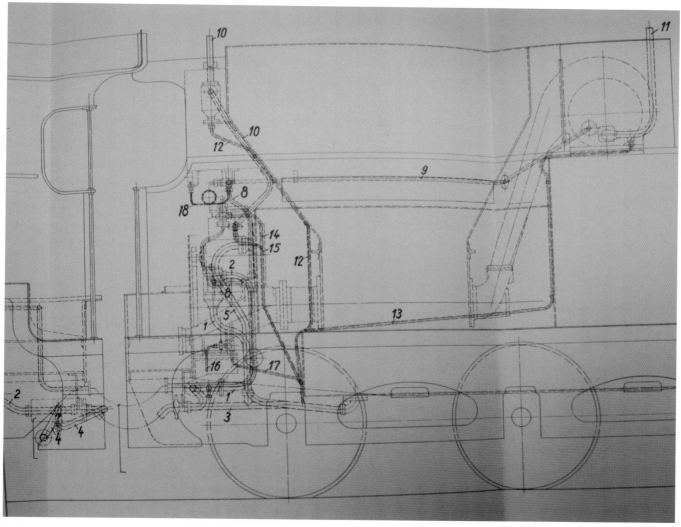

Equipment positions – note only some of these were referred to in the original text.

Care of apparatus during operation. The burners are kept free from ash and slag by means of a scraper. The ashpan can, if necessary, be cleaned of dust by lowering the ashpan bottom door. The dust in the smokebox must also be removed. The smoke and fire tubes can be cleaned by steam and compressed air blast. Should slag accumulate on the end of the superheater elements, tube ends, or nuts on the roof stays, it can be removed by careful blows with a scraper.

Interruptions in service. If the above instructions are carefully observed, no trouble need be anticipated. Nevertheless, it is just as well to point out the following difficulties which may possibly occur.

a) Stopping up of the connecting pipes with pulverised fuel. The pipes may become filled with pulverised fuel if:

i) During the fuelling, the sealing sleeves are open, or only partially closed, thus allowing fuel to escape from the fuel container through into the mixing chamber. This may also happen if the bunker is filled at too high a pressure.

ii) If one of the screws is rotating when the turbo fan is not operating.

iii) The fuel used is too moist and causes the screw to stick fast. (For instance due to water in the air pipes when filling the bunker.)

To free the connecting pipes, the following should be done. If the main connecting pipes are stopped up, the burner box is first cleared by means of compressed air from a stationary plant introduced through the inspection doors provided. The inspection cover 'W' of the mixing chamber is next removed and the pipes blown out by means of compressed air introduced into the mixing chamber. If the pipes are free, but the screw fast, the screw is rotated backwards and forwards by means of the key provided and the steam engine then put into operation. If the auxiliary burner is stopped up, cap 'M' on the small mixing chamber is removed and compressed air blown into the pipe. If this does not clear the pipe the flexible coupling between the engine and tender is removed and compressed air introduced, blowing both the pipe on the engine and the pipe on the tender clear.

b) Pulverised fuel collected in the burners. If the turbine valve steam pressure is too low, fuel may collect in the burner

Feed screws. That at bottom is at the tender end.

boxes, especially at the front end. This can be obviated by seeing that the pressure before the turbine is not lower than 42.6lbs psi when a large screw is in operation.

c) Obviating 'Turn Movement' or Breathing. To obviate tube breathing as far as possible, the chimney should be covered when no fire is burning, so that the cooling down is not too quick. It is advisable to have a small hole in the cover through which the gases which are caused by the carbonising of particles of fuel left in the firebox may escape.

Selection of turbine stop valve pressures in relation to the rpm of the auxiliary engine when both screws are being used. Having regards to the variations and condition of the fuel being used, as well as to the fact that the screws propel a different quantity of fuel when the bunker is full, as against when the bunker is empty, it is impossible to give an exact pressure at the turbine stop valve which is correct in all cases. Nevertheless, the following table taken from actual experience gives a basis to work upon.

RPM of Auxiliary Engine	Pressure at Turbine Stop Valve: Atmospheres	Pressure at Turbine Stop Valve: Lbs PSI
125	3.5	49.7
180	4.0	56.8
225	4.5	63.9
270	5.0	71.0
315	5.5	78.1
360	6.0	85.2
400	6.5	92.3
450	7.0	99.4
500	7.5	106.5

Below and opposite top: **Two final views of No A629 in its experimental form – it can only ever be described as an experiment. Seen are the crusher and bunker for storing the pulverised fuel and again No 751 (without rods) at Eastbourne.** *H C Casserley and H F Wheeler*

Seen in the background to several of the views of No A629 is the 'Terrier' No 751. The involvement of No 751 is also interesting as this was the sole member of the 'Terrier' class sold to the SECR, hence the numbering. It returned to the SR in 1923 but by this time was in poor condition and so with boiler pressure reduced to just 75psi, it found a specific use at Eastbourne in connection with No A629. Following the culmination of the pulverised fuel experiment (presumably it did not follow No A629 to Ashford?) it was repaired and later given a new boiler and survived into BR days. It was subsequently saved for preservation and as No 54 *Waddon* was presented to the Canadian Railway Museum in 1963. It is seen here at Ashford still in 'Battleship Grey' and probably awaiting repair following the termination of use in the experiments with No A629.

(As an aside, it is interesting to note how even in what was a British report the use of metric measurements is used on occasions. Something to do perhaps with the origins of the actual equipment?)

When only using one screw the stop valve pressure need only be 3-4Kg/Cm2 (42.6 to 55.9lbs psi.).

The revolution of the auxiliary engine can be read from the revolution counter 'U' provided. The turbine stop valve pressure can be read on gauge 'P'.

Perhaps the last word should be left to André Chapelon, who in his seminal work of 1952, 'La Locomotive a Vapeur', (English translation published 2000) in referring to the use of pulverised fuel states, "Despite some initial applications which were unsuccessful, the use of pulverised coal firing on locomotives has been applied effectively for some years, especially on the Reichsbahn [2 h's, not 3] after development testing of two 2-10-0s of class 'G12' which were so fitted in 1928, one with STUG equipment and the other with that from AEG. However, the satisfactory use of lignite alone must be solved, use of this coal causing major problems, especially following the rapid 'birds-nesting' of the tubes which results in the fouling up of the firebox tubeplate after running quite an inadequate distance."

From this we may conclude that lignite alone was not the sole fuel and possibly something more among the lines of a mixture, the colloidal type fuel referred to earlier, was being burnt.

Chapelon also refers to "birds nesting" whilst Holcroft of course had mentioned "molten slag". The difference here though is likely to be the result of the actual fuel being used and we know on the SR it was hard black coal rather than lignite proper.

It would be fascinating to be able to report further on No A629 and indeed on the success or otherwise of the experiments undertaken elsewhere, although in reality 'SW' should strictly confine itself to 'SR' matters. If any reader does have access to or knowledge of reports of the trials for No A629, I am sure many would be most interested.

Aside from the sources mentioned with the text, the author would also like to express his gratitude to Gerry Nichols and the library of the Stephenson Locomotive Society.

To be continued in Issue No 47.

A return to normal seen here as BR(S) No 31629 at Norwood on 3 June 1963. The chimney was 'cut off' on the original print. *Stephenson Locomotive Society*

Book Review
Colonel Stephens and his Railmotors

Years ago I remember being asked by my daughters what I would like for Christmas. Being a bit fed up with the obligatory socks, handkerchiefs and general ornaments, I decided to try a different approach and requested an 'O' gauge wagon kit from Messrs Slaters. "Ooh – where do we get that from?" asked one. "Fear not", I responded, "I will buy it, you can wrap it up and repay me". Well Christmas Day duly arrived and I feigned surprise at unwrapping exactly what it was I had asked for. Where is this going? Simply that if I were asked the same question again this time, what I would like for a present, I would have no hesitation in asking for the recent title by Brian James and Ross Shimmon on 'Colonel Stephens and his Railmotors' published at the end of 2018 by our friends at Lightmoor Press.

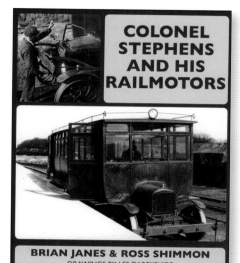

I first saw this book as a new title at the Warley show in November, too late then to mention it to readers of 'SW' as a potential Christmas gift but be assured had that knowledge been around in time it would most certainly have been mentioned – and no doubt on more than one letter to Lapland!

For fear though of anyone obtaining the wrong book for me *(other books on Col Stephens are of course available!),* I would probably also have ensured I tracked this one down myself, not least as I doubt I could have waited until the next birthday and certainly not Christmas 2019. Oh, and by the way, whilst daughters certainly got it right with the wagon kit all those years ago, I should perhaps mention how I responded when asked if I would like to select another kit as a gift the following year? To this I simply replied, "To be refunded for last year's would be nice...".(What I had deliberately failed to mention to them is that years later it is still in the drawer waiting to be built!)

'Colonel Stephens and his Railmotors' is written by Brian Janes & Ross Shimmon with drawings by Les Darbyshire. Published by Lightmoor Press in 2018, it contains 136 sides, split into nine chapters and an appendix. The book is case-bound, printed on quality art paper with excellent illustrations in b/w, many of which were certainly new to your reviewer.

Aside from the use of the various railcars on the KESR and WSR, a readable and well balanced text includes the use of such vehicles – regardless as to the method of propulsion – on the WC&P and S&M. Both passenger and freight vehicles feature. Certainly one for the bookshelf.

1 Leeds Wheel and Axle Co manufactured a new type of disc wheel patented by Mr. W H Kitson, one of the managing partners. The chief feature of the wheel is the provision of a central flange or disc, which extends from the boss nearly to the tyre, and is traversed by the bolts securing the Mansell rings. This central disc is either forged in one piece with the boss, or if a cast-iron boss is used, it is made of wrought iron plate and the boss cast on it. Found online at: https://www.gracesguide.co.uk/1876_Iron_and_Steel_Institute:_Visits_to_Works

Selsey station with the pair of Sheflex railcars and open wagon in between.

Malden Manor

We are delighted to present a very short pictorial piece on Southern concrete architecture based on four images recently acquired and from the lens of the SR official photographer.

As built for the new line from Motspur Park to Chessington, all four of the new stations displayed the same design of Chisarc cantilevered canopies with the advance they gave a platform surface free of supporting pillars. This first view is from the Tolworth direction with the constructional material – concrete of course – now obvious. The same was used for much of the other infrastructure, platform walls and edges, and the rectangular tower on the left which was intended to be a goods lift from road level but was never completed internally.

Within and at platform level at least the whole is still modern in the 21st century although nowadays the likely preferred constructional materials would probably be stainless steel and glass. The design was by James Robb Scott who had joined the LSWR in 1907 and who was heavily involved in work at Waterloo between 1909 and 1923. Scott being responsible for the office range, main entrance and Victory Arch. Aside from here he was also responsible for the stations at Ramsgate (1925), Bromley north (1925), Byfleet & New Haw (1927), Dumpton park (1928), Exmouth (1929), Wimbledon (1930), Wimbledon Chase (1930), Hastings (1931), Bishopstone (1936), Surbiton (1937), Richmond (1938), Horsham (1939), and the two Chessington stations in 1939. It should be added that certainly all were identical.

WAY OUT

Night time view with the new fluorescent lighting displayed to advantage. The Southern Railway described the architectural style as being of the 'Marine' type although later the more popular term used was 'Odeon' or more formally 'Art Deco'.

Opposite: The modern styling was not extended beyond the structure however as signage was conventional green and white enamel. Whilst visually attractive at platform level the same might not totally be said at road level, hence the need for the goods lift. Curves and form still abounded but did not necessarily form a cohesive link to the eye. (See Middleton Press '*Wimbledon to Epsom including the Chessington Branch*' image No 42 and also 49.)

The
Southern Way
The regular volume for the Southern devotee
MOST RECENT BACK ISSUES

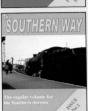
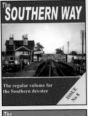

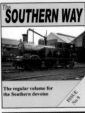

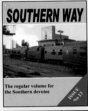
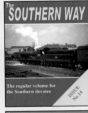

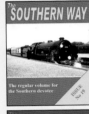

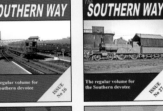
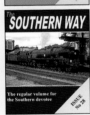
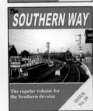

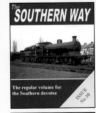

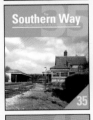
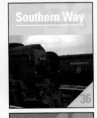

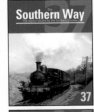

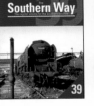
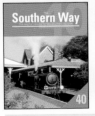
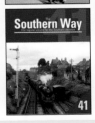
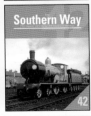
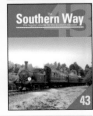

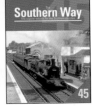

The Southern Way is available from all good book sellers, or in case of difficulty, direct from the publisher. (Post free UK) Each regular issue contains at least 96 pages including colour content.

£11.95 each
£12.95 from Issue 7
£14.50 from Issue 21
£14.95 from Issue 35

Subscription for four-issues available
(Post free in the UK)
www.crecy.co.uk